What Does it Mean to be a Liberal in India

What Does it Meaan to be a Liberal in India

First published in 2016
by

ACADEMIC FOUNDATION
4772-73 / 23 Bharat Ram Road, (23 Ansari Road),
Darya Ganj, New Delhi - 110 002 (India).
Phones : 23245001 / 02 / 03 / 04.
Fax : +91-11-23245005.
E-mail : books@academicfoundation.com
www.academicfoundation.org

in association with:
FRIEDRICH NAUMANN FOUNDATION FOR FREEDOM (FNF)
www.fnfsouthasia.org

Disclaimer:
The findings/views/opinions expressed in this book are solely those of the authors and do not necessarily reflect the views of the publisher.

Cataloging in Publication Data--DK
Courtesy: D.K. Agencies (P) Ltd. <docinfo@dkagencies.com>

What does it mean to be a liberal in India / edited by Ronald Meinardus.
pages cm
Contributed articles.
ISBN 9789332703773

1. Liberalism--India. 2. Liberty. I. Meinardus, Ronald, 1955- editor.

JC574.2.I4W43 2016 DDC 320.51954 23

Typeset, printed and bound by The Book Mint, New Delhi.
www.thebookmint.in

CONTENTS

About the Editor/Contributors

Editor:

Ronald Meinardus calls himself a liberal, a political commentator, a desk activist and a Philhellene. He moved to New Delhi in summer 2015 as the Regional Director South Asia of the Friedrich Naumann Foundation for Freedom (FNF). Before that, he served the Foundation in Egypt, the Philippines, South Korea and Greece. A journalist by profession and training, Dr Meinardus has published widely on current political affairs in academic journals and the media. Before leaving Cairo, he edited *Liberalism in the Arab World: Just a Good Idea?* (Mahrousa Publishers 2015).

Contributors:

Kalyani Subbiah (19 years) is a student of the Integrated Masters in Development Studies at Indian Institute of Technology, Madras (IIT-M) for the years 2013-2018. She won an Honourable Mention in the international "Emerging Leaders" essay competition conducted by Project Firefly and Credit Suisse, and second place for her paper on literacy at the Census Data Dissemination Workshop sponsored by UN Women. Kalyani has also written a special report on the New Silk Road for the IIT-M China Studies Centre. She has a Grade 8 (with distinction) in violin and plays in Western classical concerts with the Madras Musical Association orchestra. Apart from this, she has chaired the Security Council at IIT-M

Model United Nations and is currently the Under-Secretary-General of IITMMUN.

Karthik Shankar (25 years) is a Young India Fellow at Ashoka University for the year 2015-16. He was a writer for *The Times of India*. In addition he has also contributed to *The Hindu*, *Youth Ki Awaaz*, *South Asia Monitor*, Observer Research Foundation and Chennai Centre for China Studies. He also writes on gender issues for The Red Elephant Foundation. Karthik has been part of the daily newsletter production team for the 2013 edition of the Chennai Film Festival and was the head of the Twitter team for Lit for Life 2015, the literary festival by *The Hindu*.

Barath Balaji (18 years) is a 2nd year under graduate student of Economics at Ramakrishna Mission Vivekananda College. He was part of his school's student council and has won over 130 school and college speaking events. He was part of one among the three teams globally to win a Special Mention at the International Public Policy Forum and was selected for the Indian Debating Team try-outs twice. He has participated in several Model United Nation conferences, both as delegate and Chairperson of Committees and has a number of Best Delegate awards to his name. He was also a participant at the Young Global Citizens Summit organised by the British Council in Bhubaneswar, January 2012. He is currently the Creative Head and a Trainer at Warhorse, an educational enterprise that trains high school students in Public Speaking.

Cherryy Chauhan (19 years) is a student at Bharati Vidyapeeth's College of Engineering for the year 2013-2017. She is the current documentation head of International Society of Automation, BVP Chapter. In addition to that she also served as the Literary Captain of her school prefect board. She is currently interning with Delhi based travel website SoDelhi.com as a content writer.

Chinmaya Lal Thakur (21 years) is a Masters student in English at the University of Delhi. He is interested in studying the relationship between literature and politics. His areas of interest are the Theory of the Novel, the Nineteenth Century Novel, and modern Indian writing. He has presented several papers in national and international conferences and published in leading journals.

Diwakar Sharma (23 years) is at Motilal Nehru National Institute of Technology, Allahabad for the year 2014-2016. He is currently pursuing Master of Technology. An avid reader, he takes interest in a wide range of subjects including History, Economics and Philosophy. In addition, he is a musician. Being an artist at heart, he likes to write on interesting topics. He has participated in numerous writing competitions and has also contributed to the open page section of leading newspapers.

Harish Alagappa (27 years) currently works as a Business Development Manager with Exponential Interactive, a leading digital advertising network. He was previously an Assistant Editor with The Energy and Resources Institute (TERI), where he wrote for *Terra Green* magazine, and created, edited, and wrote for *Energy Future* magazine. In addition, he has also contributed to *Youth Ki Awaaz*, the *Encyclopaedia of Energy*, and *Sportskeeda*. Harish was part of the blog team for the 2015 edition of the Jaipur Literature Festival.

Reijul Sachdev (22 years) is in the 4th year of a 5-year Integrated MTech programme at IIIT (International Institute of Information Technology)-Bangalore. He recently completed an internship at the MIT Media Lab on the Andorra Living Lab project. He enjoys grappling with math problems and has published solutions to problems in the *American Mathematical Monthly* journal. Not just numbers, he loves words and ideas too. He has competed in and won several debates, including the Frank Anthony Memorial Debate (national champion and best speaker) and Debating Matters India by British Council (regional champion and best speaker). He appeared on TV as a national finalist of the Youth Parliament of the 'I Lead India!' initiative by *The Times of India*. In addition, he is enrolled in a Philosophy course with the New Acropolis Foundation and is a member of Greenpeace.

Harshita Lall (20 years) is at St. Stephen's College, University of Delhi for the year 2015. She has worked with Ernst and Young (EY), World Wide Fund for Nature (WWF), Federation of Indian Chambers of Commerce and Industry (FICCI) and was First Author for a research paper for national seminar at Sikkim University. In addition, she has also contributed to UK India Education and Research Initiative (UKIERI), British Council, Chief Minister's Rural Housing Scheme, Sikkim University and non-governmental organisation Making a Difference. She also works on gender issues and education for street children in India for Sarwanchal Sanskritik Avam Samajik Vikas Manch (SUDHI) . Harshita is the Director of The United Nations Youth Association of India and has served as Vice President of House of Commons Society of Sri Venkateswara College, Event Head of English Literary Association, the literary society of Sri Venkateswara College and member of Film and Photography society of Sri Venkateswara College. She also holds a Taekwondo Blue Belt. She is a two-time Gold Medallist and has won the G.V. Subramaniam Award for English as well as the Nelabhatla Venkata Subbiah Memorial Prize at Sri Venkateswara College, University of Delhi and "Excellence in Creative Writing" four years in a row at Brightlands School, India.

Jash Dholani (18 years) is a fresher at Pandit Deendayal Petroleum University. His pieces have been featured in his college magazine, the *New Indian Express*, and he has been published in a horror anthology. He dabbles freely in fiction and non-fiction, and was recently a top 10 winner in *The Times of India's* Write India contest. A public speaking aficionado, a poet, and a freestyle film maker, he is learning what it is to explore, experience and live.

N.R. Prashanth Bhat (29 years) is a graduate student at the Philip Merrill College of Journalism in the University of Maryland-College Park, USA. He worked as a reporter for *Deccan Chronicle* and *The Times of India* in Hyderabad, India. His blogs regularly appear on *The Huffington Post*. He interned with some of the leading media organisations such as *The National Geographic, China Central Television-America*, and the *Voice of America*. He was also a research intern at the Centre for Civil Society, New Delhi.

Sreyoshi Guha (20 years) is a Third Year law student at Symbiosis Law School, Pune for the years 2013-2018. She has written for *Gulf News*, UAE's leading English daily during her internship with them in 2013. She has also authored legal essays and papers, participated in competitions and conferences organised by institutions like Independent Thought and The National Commission for Women, among others. As a firm believer in the potential of today's Youth, she has also been a part of AIESEC in its Pune Chapter. In her own words, she is a closet idealist, an armchair philosopher and likes to document her thoughts in her blog: chasingambiguities.wordpress.com.

Tanmayi Gidh (19 years) is a second year student of Philosophy at Fergusson College, Pune University for the year 2015-16. She contributes to a number of student-run literary magazines and adventure websites and enjoys writing poetry. She is an ardent adventure lover, mountaineer and traveller and loves reaching out to readers about these moving experiences through her blog "The Wandering Wind", which has also been featured in *The Times of India*.

Utkarsh Srivastava (22 years) is a lawyer practising in Bombay. He is a part of the Class of 2015 of the National University of Juridical Sciences, Kolkata. He has a keen interest in writing on different issues and has contributed articles in publications like *Scroll*. His areas of interest include football, technology, feminism debates and the right to free speech.

Vageesha Sushan (20 years) is a IInd year law student in Lloyd Law College, Greater Noida. She was an avid contributor to her school's (D.A.V Public School, Cantt. Area) yearly magazine *Diksha* till the time she completed her intermediate schooling in 2013. An avid blogger, she is dedicated in her support to a number of social causes.

Vaishnavi Ray (19 years) is a senior student at Amity University Rajasthan for the year 2017, and is currently pursuing her Bachelor's degree in Computer Science. She completed her primary education with distinction from her hometown Vijayawada; and is a full term scholarship recipient even at University. She is passionate about writing, and has over a lakh views on her year-old blog, "The Rejected Lemon". In addition, Vaishnavi is the President of her college E-Magazine and the Head of the Literature Society. She is also an established Public Speaker and has launched her startup "#LifeBasics", which is a Personality Development organisation that aims at helping students with non-English Medium education history or poor financial backgrounds conquer their stage fear and prepare for interviews. Her active participation in several Street Theatre Performances (Nukkad Naatak) stands testimony to her love for social activism and drama. She has also dabbled in photography, and is an Instagram and Pinterest addict. When she isn't writing or teaching, she is reading or singing gospels for her University Choir.

Vani Manchanda (18 years) is a student at Pearl Academy University for the year 2015-2018. She is doing a professional course of interiors and architecture design from there. She is passed out from Bal Bharati School.

Prakhar Misra (23 years) is a student of Economics and Finance at the Meghnad Desai Academy of Economics and is the recipient of the Chanakya Scholarship. Prior to this, he was a Swaniti fellow before which he completed the Teach For India Fellowship. He has been a speaker and a judge at many national and international debate tournaments across India, Malaysia, Hong Kong and Bangladesh. He also contributes articles to *The Huffington Post*, *PolicyWonks.in* and *KarmanyConnect.com*. He completed a certificate in Public Policy from The Takshashila Institution and a Bachelors' in Engineering from M.S. Ramaiah Institute of Technology where he also co-founded a Social Media Marketing company-ADDO.

Rohit Balagopal (20 years), based in Kochi, is a student of law, currently studying in the third year of a five year course in the National University for Advanced Legal Studies. As a former resident of the Garden City, he endeavours to divide his time between Kochi and Bangalore. Apart from being an aspiring lawyer, he is also an avid reader, with a keen interest in international law. He also enjoys quizzing and evinces a keen interest in debating as well.

RONALD MEINARDUS

Introduction

I'll start with a confession: The idea to hold a writing competition and publish a book with the best essays was very much my own. A mixture of personal interest and you may call it strategic considerations motivated the project.

Let me begin with the personal. Like most of the fellow authors, I consider myself a liberal. Over many years, the conviction that freedom is the most important human right, a condition for good governance and economic development has matured in my mind.

My liberal 'career' started when I was a student of a major German university, where I fought it out with Communist and other Marxist groups, who—as we know—have seen their ideology punished by history. Today, I have the privilege to work for an organisation whose objective is to promote liberalism. Over the past two and a half decades, I have served in various parts of the world, in Southern Europe, East Asia, South East Asia, the Middle East and North Africa, and now, at last, in India. Throughout, promoting liberalism has been my assignment. This has been much more than a professional mandate; call it a mission, as long as you remove the religious connotation of that term.

Those of you who know my employer, the Friedrich Naumann Foundation for Freedom, will appreciate the importance of associating with local partners. These play a crucial role in all the programmes, and thus the effort to promote liberalism.

It's very rare that you'll see activities organised by the Foundation without a local partner. It is with and through the cooperation with partners that we aim to achieve our objectives. This strategic axiom also guided us in the project, the result of which you're holding in your hands.

This being an effort aimed at the young generation, we partnered with "Students for Liberty", an international network of students whose mission is to educate, develop and empower the next generation on liberty—the very essence of liberalism. The mobilising talents of our young friends helped us get the word out and achieve the reach-out for the competition. Our main institutional partner has been the Centre for Civil Society (CCS), the New Delhi based liberal think tank that has earned high grades for successful pro-liberty work and advocacy in India and beyond. My gratitude goes to our partners for the good cooperation which has produced an impressive piece of work.

As the editor of the book, I had the task and also the pleasure to read the texts multiple times. I also had the honour to work together with a team of eminent Indian Jury members, who helped select the best writings in a highly competitive and always transparent process. While they deserve recognition for their efforts, the members of the Jury asked not to be mentioned in order not to divert attention away from our young authors.

Unlike other political mainstreams, such as socialism, conservatism or religious fundamentalism, liberalism is not a closed set of ideological principles and values. The rejection of dogmatism, or—to put it positively: the openness to debate, dissent and diversity, is one of the features of liberalism. While some may misjudge this openness for randomness, it is not so at all. Liberal aspirations are always driven by the quest for more freedom for more individuals. Freedom stands at the core of liberal thinking, liberal advocacy, liberal policy design and governance. As the basic principle, it is not negotiable. Therefore, liberals have good reasons to show a lack of tolerance for those who question or curtail freedom.

To promote liberal principles in an international context, it is crucial to understand the respective political, social and cultural environment. Obviously, these vary from one country to another. It is a platitude that different societies face different challenges. However, this simple observation has significant implications for the policy debates and programmatic positioning. I have worked with liberals and liberally minded individuals and their organisations in different parts of the world. I have come across diverse understandings and definitions of liberal priorities and policies. The liberal agendas to tackle specific issues in a specific society and historic context will differ—a successful business leader in South Korea (with a Confucian background) may see liberalism differently than an unemployed Muslim student in Egypt harassed and tortured by the police. However, and importantly, both believe in the primary importance of individual freedom. Therefore, both are members of the global liberal family.

This brings me back to our book. Remarkably, India, the biggest democracy on earth, has no liberal party or major liberal political force. I have heard various explanations for the absence of organised liberalism. Also in other parts of the world, there exist only weak liberal parties or none at all. One explanation is, the citizens (and voters) of those countries don't see the need for a liberal force as they deem basic freedoms in their democracies have been attained. In general, I don't agree with this assertion; the struggle for freedom is a never ending story. Concerning India, it has no validity at all. With all the due respect for India's great democratic tradition, India's democracy is far away from providing a liberal paradise.

Where then and who are India's liberals? Related to this: what does it mean to be a liberal in India?

For institutes like mine, there exist various methodologies to find an answer. We could have commissioned a researcher to investigate the matter and provide another study to enrich the sociological bibliography. We chose an alternate approach which I find more direct, honest and appropriate. We asked those with a position and an opinion (and knowledge) themselves. Thus, was born the idea of the essay writing competition.

The call for submissions has had an extremely pleasing response. Not only were we overwhelmed by the sheer quantity of entries. Even more pleasing has been the quality of many of the writings. For me, reading these texts has been a learning experience of the special kind. Importantly, it has given me an answer to the query of what it means to be liberal in India.

For my fellow members of the jury, all of them high power liberal and intellectual minds in their own right, it has been an agonising exercise to trim down the entries to the small selection of winning contributions we are publishing in this book.

We believe, the ensuing works reflect the richness and diversity of liberal thought in this country. The book mirrors the intellectual ingenuity and power of young Indians who aspire for more freedom for themselves, but importantly also their community and their nation.

While India may be void of a liberal political party, many of her people agree that the huge challenges facing the country will only be overcome by granting more freedom and not less. Freedom, tolerance and secularism are a safeguard for India's unique cultural, religious and political diversity. More economic freedom is the most effective way to unleash the power of the markets and lead hundreds of millions Indians out of poverty at last.

You'll find more such liberal arguments in the ensuing pages. I am aware such positioning will raise much argument. That is exactly one of the objectives of this book. The Foundation and her partners will use the texts to engage Indian liberals and others in a political dialogue. We welcome you to join the debate.

Meanwhile, I invite you to lean back and enjoy reading this stimulating book.

1

KALYANI SUBBIAH

Sexual Illiberalism in the Indian Society

Introduction: Kiss of Love

On a humid evening in Chennai, a motley group of students nervously gather around the entrance of the Indian Institute of Technology, Madras, to hold their 'Kiss of Love' protest. Demanding the right to public displays of affection without harassment by the police, media or fundamentalist groups, they hug or kiss each other in couples in front of assembled press cameras. This protest is sensationalised by the local media and lapped up with amusement by the public. Public reactions vary from the victorious liberal, to uncomfortable conservative-centre youth, openly furious Hindutva party workers and a public majority that chooses to skirt understanding the protests or simply consumes the event as a detestable spectacle without engaging in debate.

Hence, with a lack of public engagement and support in the issue, the protestors faced open opposition from fundamentalist religious groups who threatened and harassed them. This incident reflects the reality of the liberal situation in India, where a highly liberal minority is pitted against a conservative majority. The liberal in Indian society is despised by the majority of the populace for threatening what they view as the very fabric of Indian society: caste and religious homogeneity supported by the institution of arranged marriage, regulation of gender norms and a variety of social practices that they view part of an Indian 'culture' superior to that of the Western other.

Liberalism, Westernisation and Wealth: Intersections

Liberal/conservative views are fractured on the lines of age, education and wealth. Young, wealthy graduates of the social sciences are the most likely to be liberal in the complete sense, accepting homosexuality—which one could say is the pinnacle of liberal perspective. Other young, educated people are partially ushered into a liberal viewpoint by Western news media, films, songs, or segments of the increasingly liberal English domestic news media and Bollywood movies. The latter crowd at most times accepts the portrayal of open heterosexuality and rejects casteism, which is a start though not entirely 'liberal'. Apart from these social groups, there is a small section of highly educated intellectuals (often in the social sciences) who espouse and engage in liberal activism. The majority of the populace, however, is stridently conservative in opinion, especially on issues of love and sexual relations.

The intersection of wealth, Westernisation and a liberal perspective means that the liberals are often derided as elitist and portrayed as degenerate—people who have forgotten their 'roots'. The Westernisation of the elite is mocked regularly in vernacular media, and the local culture, language and moral perspective are regularly valorised as ideal as opposed to Western culture which is portrayed as the 'other': alien, invasive and immoral. For some, exposure to Western media—increasing news of divorces, mass shootings, and racism in the West and the portrayal of sexuality in cinema—has further hardened their stance against liberalism and for the protection of Indian culture, constructed as asexual and 'moral'. The elite liberals are added to the 'other' of the West against which notions of nationality and cultural pride are constructed or are portrayed as thoughtless followers of Western culture/traitors of Indian culture.

Sexual Illiberalism and the Dangerous Figure of the Liberal

Debates on liberalism are structured around the social context of countries. While in China, several debates revolve around political liberalism and democracy, in India, a democracy but—the land of arranged marriages and closed communities of caste and religion—sexual liberalism dominates the debates. Each caste forms a community of its own with different cultural practices, social norms, and prejudices and opinions of the other, hence caste mixing is likely to result in loss of caste-specific traditions, and confusions of status. The specific hierarchies of caste and notions of purity means that one type of marriage: caste hypogamy or a high caste female marrying a low caste man is highly taboo and rigorously punished. This is because a community's honour and purity is located in the female body, with religious notions of the purity of the woman's womb being sullied by a lower caste. Further, a lower caste husband would bring down the status of the family, while marrying up is preferred (though caste hierarchies can be more complex with two or more antagonistic castes all on the same socio-economic level but with different notions of superiority).

Inter-religious marriage comes with similar challenges on an even greater scale. From a functionalist perspective, to maintain caste homogeneity, the institution of arranged marriage functions well. Hence love out of volition before marriage is banned or strictly regulated, making up the base for a conservative society—where female behaviour and spaces are heavily regulated, and transgressions are punished with social ostracisation or in an extreme manner (sometimes) honour killings. The liberal views on sexual freedom and the liberty to love expressed in national/local debates, acted out on live news channels, newspapers and social media hence threaten to rework the very fabric of Indian society, that is based on same-caste kin relations. Therefore, the figure of the liberal is viewed as dangerous and immoral by the majority of the populace.

These complex norms surrounding love before marriage co-exist with other norms regarding the portrayal of sexuality in public, which is strictly banned. Sexuality is relegated to the secrecy of bedrooms of the married and is refused expression in any other space or time, save certain media such as cinema and television. As in most other societies, children are not exposed to sexuality, and media is graded according to permissible levels of sexuality. With the censor board becoming more lenient, public opinion of the older generation and religious groups is that cinema is 'corrupted'. In popular discourse (especially vernacular media), society is depicted as being in a progressive decline from a state of 'decent' regulated sexuality to 'indecent' or immoral open sexuality, aided by the influence of mass media. The use of 'decent' serves as a euphemism for a kind of ascetism about sexuality and lack of perceived misbehaviour, often involving an open display of asexuality: dressing in unglamorous clothes that cover all the parts of the body considered appropriate, and a reserved behaviour. For example, an upper-class neighbourhood sans slums, wine shops, and prostitute dens is described as 'decent'. Often decency is conflated with upper-caste, upper-class characteristics. In such a society, liberal intellectuals who espouse views in support of less sexual or other regulation—reducing harassment of sex workers, allowing pubs to be open without harassing customers, allowing women to wear their clothes of choice without being blamed for inviting rape, reducing regulations on the portrayal of sexuality in books and media, free love—risk being seen as immoral or 'indecent'. Such a tag can be damaging in a society that places high value on even the 'morality' of its film stars.

Liberalism and the Indian Woman

Over the decades in India, questions of liberalism have revolved almost neurotically around the female body and persona. When the male population began wearing suits and hats, and going to work, no-one batted an eye. The spirit of the nation, with its culture and its differentiation from the colonial 'other' from which it emerged victorious, was situated in the woman. Women were already straddled with the strict restrictions on behaviour imposed by the fear of caste hypogamy: with restrictions increasing as caste status increased. Now, the new nation's honour and pride was situated in 'Mother India' and vicariously in the traditional woman who stayed at home, and embodied Indian culture in attire and reserved behaviour. Hence, female honour became an increasing source of anxiety for Indian society as it no longer just embodied the honour of the community, but also the honour and character of the new nation. Several nationalist plays pre-independence mocked the promiscuousness of the Westernised woman and portrayed the traditional woman as saintly, asexualised and Goddess-like, a practice that continues in movies and popular soap operas to this day. The upper-caste, upper-class, traditional heroine in soap operas is regularly portrayed as a symbol of virtue, innocence and chastity. She is contrasted with the lower-caste, low-class woman and with the Westernised woman both of whom are portrayed as 'indecent' and immoral. Hence, female attire and behaviour is expected to conform to traditional upper-caste expectations and any transgression is punished: by authorities in schools, colleges and families and/or by ostracisation and the 'gaze' of society in public. Women are judged by higher standards than men on behaviour, dress and attributes such as consumption of alcohol and tobacco and the constant disciplining inculcates a carceral culture among women who reinforce these norms on other women. Yet, the situation is not static, with women constantly negotiating and redefining their boundaries, and the gradual spread of Westernisation and liberalism among upper-class youth has well softened stringent regulations among the elite. This is, however, at times met with a backlash by the conservative section of society due to the influence of conservative opinion that sees the need to protect supposedly threatened 'Indian' values.

Debating as a Liberal: Popular Liberal Arguments and their Flaws

As a counter-narrative, liberal intellectuals have attempted to portray the perceived asexuality of Indian culture as a colonial construction, pointing to examples of Hinduism's liberal portrayal and the pervasiveness of sexuality in the ancient past, the most popular being the Khajuraho temples and the Kama Sutra. Yet, while this is an effective argument as it defeats the opposition's claim at it fundamentals, it risks exclusion of minority groups like Muslims by adopting the same line of thought as Hindutva—looking to history. Further, what if India had a sexually repressive past? Would then the present have to be so? Hence, the liberal making a cultural relativist argument finds herself on thin ice and turns to the universalist argument of liberalism, yet is defeated by a justifiable opposition that points out the Western biases in her stance, turning her once again into the figure of the traitor who abandoned Indian culture. Hence, the Indian liberal is torn between the cultural relativist and universalist stances, neither of which form satisfactory arguments, nor offer satisfactory lenses: one through history and the other through abstraction.

Many liberals hence turn to utilitarianism for their arguments: What is the best solution for social welfare? What reduces suffering and increases happiness? Yet, they once again find themselves on thin ice. Taking the example of free love, many supporters of arranged marriage point out that India has a much lower divorce rate than Western countries. Hence, liberals have to turn to contentious arguments of rights to individual choice, a fundamentally Western argument that has been constantly proved to be limited. The same applies for prevention of sex work: while many activists argue that jailing sex workers only adds to their misery and harassment, society points to the low-class background of these women, the spread of sexual diseases and their supposed suffering. In fact, liberals themselves do not form a homogenous group and are fractured around several lines based on the priorities they seek to address and the theoretical lens through which they view Indian society. While the citizen-liberal is most concerned with the norms that affect his or her immediate context, such as keeping bars open or dressing by choice or censorship of films, the intellectual-liberal is concerned with juggling equity and liberalism, focusing on caste and gender biases. Moderate liberals seek middle ground between what is perceived as Indian culture and Western culture, arguing for gradual and equitable change. But total liberals seek fulfillment of all their ideals, since they believe that the status quo is inherently unjust, especially for women, the queer and people of lower castes.

For any liberal in India, a real danger lurks: liberal activism can lead to a counter-argument that the liberal does not focus on the 'real' problems of society which are usually poverty, development and so on. She or he is accused of detracting focus from these issues and focusing on upper-class problems that supposedly hold no relevance for the lower classes intent on survival. Liberals in such a situation often hold up liberalism as the key to development, arguing that an end to skewed gender norms, caste discrimination, and so on will lead to a more equitable society, and that free speech and expression will promote lively debate and make a better democracy.

Conclusion: A Belief in Individual Choice as an End

However, a belief in liberalism in some manner entails a faith in the values of liberalism themselves without being concerned of its ends. Liberalism espouses the fundamental need to enable humans the right to live with volition: choose their sexuality, behaviour, clothes, partners and so on without repression. Yet, at the same time, it defines limits to choice where it harms others. Hence, the framework of liberalism is a perfect mixture of individualism and necessary utilitarianism. Most Indian norms however dictate that the individual's decisions are situated with the family and greater community as it affects kin relations, yet the logical fallacy of this argument that constructs a social order based innately on caste and religious discrimination is gradually being exposed. Why would one be afraid of free love if not for the fear of marrying a person from the 'wrong' community? Hence, Indian sexual illiberalism has at its heart discrimination that is slowly coming undone with the forces of urbanisation and modernisation.

The indisputable rationality of liberalism is attracting larger portions of Indian society, especially the young who are better exposed to globalisation trends. As liberal society brings more people into its fold, it is likely to gain greater clout. While this may intensify conflict between the liberal and the fundamentalist, a strong rising liberal community may shape public opinion until the liberal figure may, in society's eyes, transform from troublemaker to revolutionary.

2

KARTHIK SHANKAR

The Disgruntled Liberal

In January this year, I was part of an audience at a literature festival where the topic of discussion was the revered Tamil writer Perumal Murugan. A prolific novelist, he had announced his 'death' on Facebook after a translated version of his book had raked up controversy for its description of a couple partaking in a religious sexual ritual (Lal, 2015).

The book had the notorious distinction of riling up several different groups simultaneously. Political parties were furious for its description of Machiavellian caste politics. Hindu outfits were furious that Murugan had set the ritual in a real-life famous temple. Tamil literature aficionados were furious that he had defiled the great literary traditions of Tamil writing. Moral puritans objected to the sordid details of a private act. In the midst of this unfolding drama, all that the famous personalities who sat on stage could do was wax eloquent about Murugan's genius and express solidarity with him. All of us in the audience nodded appreciatively to the declarative statements espousing artistic freedom. Yet, deep inside we knew none of it mattered. Murugan was in a long line of liberal thinkers and intellectuals whose voices were silenced every day in our country.

Being a liberal in India means taking a stance that is in dissonance with our country's current political, social, and economic structures. The government extends the long fingers of bureaucracy into almost every aspect of our lives. Article 377 of our Constitution, a remnant of the British colonial era, uses an outdated definition of unnatural sex to criminalise homosexuality. The Armed Forces Special Powers Act grants extra-judicial powers to the army in vaguely described 'disturbed areas'. Police in the state of Kerala even arrested shopkeepers selling Bob Marley t-shirts under a head-scratcher of a law called Young Persons (Harmful Publications) Act, 1956 (Firstpost, 2014).

Individual autonomy seems like a pipe dream in the India I live in. We are shooed away by policemen from public spaces after a certain time in the night. We are patted down, frisked and have our baggage scanned even while entering a mall or using the metro. There's this belief that national security trumps all concerns and in the process the state is venerated and the individual belittled.

Liberalism: The Indian Way

But that leads into the age old question. How do we define liberalism? Who falls under the category of a liberal? As Steven Wall (2015) says in *The Cambridge Companion to Liberalism*, the word resists easy description. Moreover he asks us to view liberalism not as a single political tradition but multiple political traditions. One commonality exists though—liberals usually oppose tyranny of some sort and champion constitutional government as the fortress in this fight against tyranny.

K.R. Popper's (2013) classic work *The Open Society and its Enemies* also has the answers. Published after the end of the Second World War in two volumes, it is considered by many to be one of the strongest contributions to democratic liberalism. Popper strongly advocates individualism but he also proposes that institutions must be constructed for the sole purpose of ameliorating injustice.

With regards to the Indian context, historian Ramachandra Guha (2001) astutely surmises in his paper: "The Absent Liberal" that, "Indian liberalism was a sensibility rather than a theory, a product of empirical engagement rather than an elaboration of principles laid down in canonical texts." This seems to be useful in viewing India's tradition of liberalism.

Liberalism's Past and Evolution in India

One of India's beloved history makers is Ram Mohan Roy, the founder of the influential Brahmo Samaj movement which aimed to abolish outdated religious practices like *sati*. Roy, a firebrand has been christened the first liberal. He was a vociferous advocate for the role of the state in achieving social change (Mandal and Behera, 2015). India's brand of liberalism clearly differentiated from the neo-classical liberalism that was common during the formative political conversations of the West in the start.

That tradition was carried on even after Independence by people like Nehru who championed and strengthened democratic institutions even while pursuing what some would call a misguided socialist economic policy (DNA, 2014). Guha notes that despite differences in ideology in newly independent India, there was a commitment to liberal values such as democracy, free press and independent judiciary across the board.

Somewhere in the 1970s, with the rise of Mao's China and Indira Gandhi's increasing dictatorial tendencies, liberal thought got squeezed in the polarisation between the left and the right (Ranjan, 2002). Liberalism became associated with the bourgeoisie. It neither engaged with the religious sentiments of the right or the caste identity politics of the left.

Unfortunately that continues today. None of the political parties across the ideological spectrum can claim to be bastions of liberalism. Right wing parties are caught up in their mantra to reclaim the country's Hindu heritage and curb civil liberties that emanate out of secularism. One need only to look at the recent beef ban in Maharashtra as an example which belongs to that rarest of Venn diagrams—food and freedom (Firstpost, 2015).

The left wing on the other hand tries to impose a doctrine structured by Marx whose only purpose is to consolidate the power of the state over its people. West Bengal despite all its political upheavals in recent years has essentially been a battle ground between Marxists of various hues (Mittal, 2014).

All that's left in the middle are ailing parties like the erstwhile behemoth Congress. The party is a far cry from its glory days with Nehru at the helm. Having several prominent leaders involved in a pogrom that targeted Sikhs after the assassination of Indira Gandhi and becoming synonymous with large scale corruption excludes any claims of upholding liberalism.

The Dying Dinosaur: Liberalism in Today's India

The problem in our country is that liberalism is now associated with disconnected intellectualism and both are seen as opposed to a particularly virulent strain of dogmatic conservatism. As Aiyar (1985) says in his paper, "The Concept of Liberalism and its Relevance for India", liberalism has now taken on the mantle of a political ideology rather than a philosophical concept. This enabled the philosophy to come under a three pronged attack. The first made religious or caste identity intrinsic to nationalism. The second harnessed terrorism as the boogeyman to constrain rights under the guise of national or internal security. The third and arguably the cleverest has been pitting liberalism as a threat to development.

The Religious Noose

Religion has always occupied the highest place of honour in Indian society and one of the clearest ways of defining a collective cultural identity, a tradition that continues unabated. Later on caste was also further delineated when leaders like B.R. Ambedkar and Jyotirao Phule railed against the evils of the caste system. They empowered a sizable number of people to shun the societal status conferred on them by their castes.

While all of these are no doubt welcome moments in our cultural history, liberalism is stifled under the garb of religion or caste. Murugan's book was first protested by his Gounder community. Similarly, the outcry against the banning of Wendy Doniger's supposedly incendiary polemic against Hindus illustrates the manner in which our country deals with attacks on freedom of speech (The Indian Express, 2014). Doniger's book was a marked counter to the homogenous religious tradition of Hinduism put forth by far right parties such as the Sangh Parivar and the Rashtriya Swayamsewak Sangh (RSS). The lawsuit filed against Doniger's book invoked Section 295 which criminalises "deliberate and malicious acts intended to outrage religious feelings of any class of citizens." It's a stark reminder of how the religious right has become adept at using the traditions of liberalism to push their own orthodox viewpoints.

As Jonathan Shainin (2014) of the New Yorker said in a response to the incident, "the underlying problem for free speech in India today is not simply religious intolerance but weak institutions that are incapable of upholding liberal values."

In such an environment, the only recourse liberals have is to retreat or coat their liberal ideology with heavy doses of religion, culture or nationalism. Rather than dismantle the shackles of religion itself, liberal values are justified by arguing that any intolerant ideas that emerge from religion have been wrongly derived. This is a practice rooted in our country's history starting with Roy himself. His intellectual arguments against entrenched religious practices regressed. While early on he appealed to reason, his later polemics were rooted in reinterpreting the scriptures. Some suspect this was part of Roy's tactic to reform as an insider than be seen as the incendiary outsider (Sarkar, 1975).

It continues even today. For instance Muslim women fighting for gender equality in Indian courts have used reinterpretations of Sharia law to put their point across (McIlvaine, 2014). All this exposes a key flaw in our country's political debate. Liberalism has to been seen as part of the cultural context and not for its very nature of affirming human autonomy.

Security Trumps All

One of the most popular ways that has been used to drive home this point of the disconnected liberal is national security which has assumed jingoistic tones especially when Pakistani involvement is suspected in a terror attack (and it's usually the first assumption that our government and law enforcement agencies make).

It's no surprise then that the term has become an umbrella under which multiple rights are restricted if not outright snatched. It usually starts with dispossessing a group of their national identity, which disproportionately happens in the case of Muslims, as seen in the 1983 Nellie massacre (Krishnan, 2015). Then that question of allegiance is transposed to liberals. Any liberal that takes a position that emphasises human rights, even in complicated cases, gets immediately branded as Pakistan sympathisers. Those who opposed the execution of Yakub Memon, one of the executors of the deadly 1993 Mumbai blasts, were referred to as traitors by BJP leaders (The Hindu, 2015). Last year on the heels of the Muzzafarnagar riots in Uttar Pradesh, the state government imposed a blackout on two news channels for their criticism of the ruling party (Press Trust of India, 2014).

Development *versus* Liberalism

Arguably the biggest masterstroke has been the manner in which liberalism has come to be seen as a hindrance to economic growth. Social movements like the Narmada Bachao Andolan which opposed the displacement of the economically disadvantaged due to the construction of dams on the river Narmada petered out. The popular narrative increasingly became driven by this idea of social crusaders who opposed progressive economic growth (The Telegraph, 2008).

Even earlier this year the response after the government froze the foreign funds of several NGOs, including Greenpeace and the Ford Foundation was alarming (Press Trust of India, 2015). One noticeable trend among the NGOs that were targeted was how many of them were involved with social justice related to environmentalism. The voices for the disenfranchised were silenced in one swoop.

The Failure of Liberalism in Modern India

One also has to place the blame on liberals themselves. Liberalism has transmogrified in our country though. The polarisation of politics has also led to a marked change in kind of 'liberal' thought that is being espoused. Liberalism is supposed to be about moderate political and social reform, not the upheaval of a state. Yet, the new age adherents of liberal philosophy tend to have a proclivity for libertarianism, even if they don't know it themselves.

Gurucharan Das, a self-proclaimed liberal in the public limelight is one such example. His book *India Grows at Night* makes the case for a commonly held belief, that the private sector in India has sprouted despite the bumbling government that stands in its way. Das seems to be inspired by Friedrich Hayek's striking if flawed 'spontaneous order' theory (Linker, 2014) which seems to have become a go-mantra for many new age liberals in India. The theory posits that individuals when left to their own devices will spontaneously form a social and economic order. All of these individuals conveniently ignore the role the government has played in fuelling the IT services boom or the country's economic transformation (Pant, 2015).

Sadly Das's views aren't far off from those expressed by most of the urban middle class. There's this implicit belief that the wealth we have amassed has been the result of our efforts rather than the entrenched system of unequal distribution of wealth. Is it any wonder that many in my generation think that the government is disposable? The government is seen as largely inefficient and corrupt, far from a bastion of liberalism. Conversely there are the circles of the economic elite which subscribes to the notion that the reason that China grows faster than India is because their autocracy affords them a degree of control that is not possible in our heterogeneous country. There seems to be no middle ground between a government that controls all aspects of our life and a non-existent one.

The Way Forward

Grim tales aside it's unlikely that in a country as large and heterogeneous as India, liberal traditions could die out. Yet, there needs to be a stronger consolidation of Indian liberals in the political sphere as a response to the totalitarianist elements that have sprung up in our democracy. This will require moving across party lines and that of course isn't an easy task.

A professor of mine, Jonathan Gil Harris, relayed his thoughts on the current social climate in the country. He explained that the critical reaction to any of his political opinions fell into two camps—one side embraced everything he said as an 'enlightened' foreigner. The other defenestrated his 'colonial' everything he represented. "Where's the middle ground?" Harris asked. Trust me. That's the question on the mind of every liberal in this country.

Bibliography

Aiyar, S. (1985). "The Concept of Liberalism and its Relevance for India", *Freedom and Dissent, Democratic Research Service*. Retrieved 31 August 2015 from: *indiapolicy.org/debate/Notes/aiyar.doc*

DNA (2014). "India's First PM Jawaharlal Nehru would have Hailed the India of the 21st Century", *DNA*, 27 May. Retrieved 5 September 2015 from *http://www.dnaindia.com/analysis/editorial-dnaedit-india-s-first-pm-jawaharlal-nehru-would-have-hailed-the-india-of-the-21st-century-1991487*

Firstpost (2014). "Kerala Police Crack Why Teenagers do Drugs: Blame Bob Marley", *Firstpost*, 14 March. Retrieved 26 August 2015 from *http://www.firstpost.com/living/kerala-police-crack-why-teenagers-do-drugs-blame-bob-marley-1434353.html*

———. (2015). "Beef Banned in Maharashtra: Five Years Jail, Rs 10,000 for Possession and Sale", *Firstpost*, 3 March. Retrieved 29 August 2015 from *http://www.firstpost.com/india/beef-banned-in-maharashtra-five-years-jail-rs-10000-for-possession-and-sale-2132555.html*

Guha, R. (2001). "The Absent Liberal: An Essay on Politics and Intellectual Life", *Economic and Political Weekly*, 15-21 December. Retrieved 17 August 2015 from *http://www.jstor.org/stable/4411478*

Krishnan, S. (2015). "Thirty-Two Years Later, the Nellie Massacre Remains All But Forgotten", *Caravan Magazine*, 18 February. Retrieved 29 August 2015 from *http://www.caravanmagazine.in/vantage/thirty-two-years-later-nellie-massacre-remains-all-forgotten*. See more at *http://www.caravanmagazine.in/vantage/thirty-two-years-later-nellie-massacre-remains-all-forgotten#sthash.iEv4uHQw.dpuf.*

Lal, A. (2015). "Tamil Suthor Perumal Murugan Announces his 'Death' on Facebook Over Lack of Freedom of Speech", *The Indian Express*, 15 January. Retrieved 12 August 2015 from *http://indianexpress.com/article/india/india-others/forced-to-withdraw-novel-tamil-author-announces-his-death/*

Linker, D. (2014). "Libertarianism's Terrible, Horrible, No Good, Very Bad Idea", *The Week*, 26 September. Retrieved 3 September 2015 from *http://theweek.com/articles/443462/libertarianisms-terrible-horrible-no-good-bad-idea*

Mandal, M.M. and S.K. Behera (2015). "Raja Ram Mohan Roy as an Educational Reformer: An Evaluation", *International Journal of Humanities & Social Science Studies*.January. Retrieved 14 August 2015 from *http://www.ijhsss.com/files/Mr_90be5144.-Madan-Mohan-Mandal---Dr.-Santosh-Kumar-Behera.pdf*

McIlvaine, H. (2014). "Indian Women Use Sharia Law to Fight for Gender Equality in Court System", *The Huffington Post*, 7 May. Retrieved 28 August 2015 from *http://www.huffingtonpost.com/2014/05/06/indian-women-sharia-law-gender-equality_n_5274519.html?ir=India&adsSiteOverride=in*

Mittal, T. (2014). "From Marx to Modi in West Bengal?", *Al Jazeera*, 27 May. Retrieved 21 August 2015 from *http://www.aljazeera.com/indepth/features/2014/05/from-marx-modi-west-bengal-201452711380973919.html*

Pant, S. (2015). "The Government's Contribution to the Start-up Boom in India", *BizEnablr*, 10 July Retrieved 4 September 201 from *http://bizenablr.com/index.php?route=blog/blog&blog_id=456*

Popper, K. (2013). *The Open Society and its Enemies*. Princeton: Princeton University Press.

Press Trust of India (2014). "Blackout of Two News Channels in UP, I&B Minister Promises Action", *New18*, 14 January. Retrieved 8 September 2015 from *http://www.news18.com/news/uttar-pradesh/blackout-of-two-news-channels-in-up-ib-minister-promises-action-327314.html*

———. (2015). "Foreign Funding: Govt Cancels Licences of Nearly 9,000 NGOs", *The Indian Express* 28 April. Retrieved 15 September 2015 from *http://indianexpress.com/article/india/govt-cancels-licences-of-nearly-9000-ngos/* See more at *http://indianexpress.com/article/india/govt-cancels-licences-of-nearly-9000-ngos/#sthash.eQpt7CtI.dpuf*

Ranjan, N. (2002). "Liberalism and Identity Politics", *Economic and Political Weekly*, January. Retrieved 29 August 2015 from *http://www.jstor.org/stable/4411635*

Sarkar, S. (1975). "Rammohun Roy & the Break with the Past", in P. Joshi (ed.), *Rammohun Roy and the Process of Modernization*. Vikas Publishing House. pp. 64-65.

Shainin, J. (2014). "Why Free Speech Loses in India", *The New Yorker*, 13 February. Retrieved 8 September 2015 from *http://www.newyorker.com/news/news-desk/why-free-speech-loses-in-india*

The Hindu (2015). "Anyone who Seeks Reprieve for Yakub is a Traitor", *The Hindu*, 28 July. Retrieved 8 September 2015 from *http://www.thehindu.com/news/cities/kolkata/anyone-who-seeks-reprieve-for-yakub-is-a-traitor/article7471680.ece*

The Indian Express. (2014). "Law for Bad Behaviour", *The Indian Express*, 21 February. Retrieved 7 September 2015 from *http://indianexpress.com/article/opinion/columns/law-for-bad-behaviour/*

The Telegraph. (2008). "Goddesses of All Causes", *The Telegraph*, 7 September. Retrieved 15 September 2015.

Wall, S. (2015). *The Cambridge Companion to Liberalism*. Cambridge: Cambridge University Press.

3

BARATH BALAJI

What is it to be a Liberal in India

What is liberalism? The idea of being free forms the classic side of it. The concept of equality takes the social side of it. Liberalism could be seen in more ways than these. When one says the word they could mean social liberalism, trade liberalism, political liberalism, cultural liberalism or at the most individual level, personal liberty. In India, the roots of liberalism in politics and for liberals began in 1910 with the Liberal Party of India. So what was it be a liberal at that point? Liberals were the ones who weren't fond of Congress' way of approach. For them, the INC had too many extremists. The Liberal Party was openly against British Imperialism but more moderate. They preferred to ease into independence through cooperation and constitutional reforms. But under the severe oppression of the British, this wasn't a very popular approach. The party died out after Independence and this started the unfavourable times for liberals in India.

Its quite frustrating to be a liberal in India. With a heavily right winged ideology in power and not the best of a public image, liberals face an uphill battle. This concept of 'being liberal' has always been uncomfortable here. We may be the biggest democracy in the world. The words "Liberty of thought, expression, belief, faith and worship" may be an integral part of our Preamble. But the idea of liberty is quite alien and liberals are often termed 'anti-nationalist' or 'anti-Indian'. The few that find it to the marvellous concept it is are seen obnoxious/pretentious. But why is it so? To understand that, we must break down the different kinds of liberalism and see how each play in this nation.

Classical liberalism sought to achieve complete liberty in politics and in the economy. That is something that sounds fantastic and is agreed upon on paper but quite impossible to materialise in India. In reality, the lines between church and the state often become blurred. It is quite evident that there lies bias in our decisions and we do not treat every part of the society the same way. The reason behind this is that religion and caste-ism play an integral role for a political party. Our leaders want to support equality but these vote banks are far too lucrative an option for them.

On the economic front, a liberal found no hope till 1990. That was when India adopted the LPG policies giving some respite to the liberals. But even then it was not due to a change in our beliefs but because we were strong armed by other nations to open up our doors and our economy desperately needed their help. Liberalisation of the economy has worked fantastically but there is very little to take from it as many still feel the need to restrict it. The reason behind is quite fair too. The more liberal an economy is, the more it's affected by market forces. A liberal economy does not have the government intervening. But this leads to economic disparity as not everyone in society is born equal in terms of wealth. Being a mixed economy, India heavily relies on government intervention for helping the poor. This falls directly on the face of economic liberalists.

Inequality in society destroys the essence of social liberalism. This concept stands for the same as the classic outlook but also expects societal equality. A liberal in India would find this hard to achieve as the gap between the 'haves' and 'have nots' is ever increasing. Our best solution for bridging the gap between several classes and castes involves differential treatment which defeats the entire purpose. Equality is a dream that we are far from achieving. With a plethora of communities and sub-communities, a liberal always faces the wrath of some of them whilst demanding for equal treatment.

Now India might be further behind on these accounts when compared to other countries. But inequality is a global issue. It requires a universal overhaul to impact an effective change even in a particular country. But what is highly subjective for each country and is very much in the hands of its people is cultural liberty. The country has surpassed leaps and bounds and has become a lot more open minded. But certain cultural barriers still exist. Recent bans on several kinds of meat in a few states go to show that we aren't quite open minded yet. One would expect a country to be more accepting over the decades, but moral policing still exists. People are still judged for every decision which doesn't fall in line with our archaic norms. Liberalism in India is like getting a tattoo; people like the idea of being able to do as you wish but feel guilty using this ability. The country wants to advance but is quite unsure whether it'll be able to handle the changing cultures.

That brings us to the final aspect, personal liberty. On paper, we have complete liberty to do anything that does not cause third party harms or isn't generally accepted as immoral. But the problem in this lies with the fact that these parameters are highly subjective. Though legally we could say or do what we want in India, the restrictions exist on a psychological level. Our society isn't ready to accepts freedom of expression yet. People often keep their opinions to themselves for fear of backlash. An example is the case of author Perumal Murugan who gave up writing due to the severe opposition he faced for his works. Any topic that might go against public opinion or established cultural and religious facts are shunned (sometimes violently). Even opinions on the Internet are heavily scrutinised leading to the arrest of people for posting their opinions online. The Supreme Court had to remove the law 66A recently to ensure people don't get incarcerated for their opinions. Not only do liberals here have to thrive in these poor situations, the treatment towards them too are considered hostile. They are popularly satirised for being obnoxious and having double standards. People blow them away as being overzealous.

But the liberals themselves could be blamed for the status quo. Being free, they've never really had one cohesive voice. With each person understanding liberalism in different ways and drawing subjective lines of freedom, the entire concept has been quite misunderstood. There has been no actual impact that the liberals have made on others as their arena for discussion is merely social networking debates. The problem sometimes is more underlying where people do not really understand what it is when they call themselves a liberal. They merely are impressed by the sheen the western liberals have.

Now the good thing about India is that we are not regressing. True, it is quite frustrating to be a liberal in India, but things have improved quite a bit. Despite radical parties holding power, they are mellowed down with the slow inclination of the general public towards moderate leaders. Western influences are often seen to be culture eroding, but they have merely opened our minds by showing what it means to be a more accepting society.

4

CHERRYY CHAUHAN

Liberal Hypocrisy

Ancient Indians were so clever about achieving the perfect way for sexual gratification that they went on to write a whole book about it. They also went on to create a Mars mission with a budget lesser than it took to make the movie *Gravity*. Indians are many, of course, owing to the one billion people residing in this wonderful nation I'm proud to call India, but they are definitely far more fascinating than they might seem.

A nation can't be called liberal if its people are imposed with restrictions and do not have the agency to follow their own minds and do what they like or think as they want. India for one is a diverse nation both by cultural and geographical aspects. The Preamble of the Indian Constitution is a token of the prudent way it is designed with respect to the liberty of the citizens. It gives us the "liberty of thought, expression, belief, faith and worship". And there, in just one line the whole perspective of India over liberty was pretty much summed up.

The term 'liberal' is often analogous with the term 'freedom' which is nothing but the power to write, act or speak as a person desires without any intervention from the state or the society. When asked on his views over 'liberty', Robert Frost, one of the most celebrated poets of our generation winningly quoted that, "A liberal is a man too broad minded to take his own side in a quarrel." Mr Frost brilliantly captured the essence of the word liberal by merely quoting the obvious. Abiding by the spirit of his words, liberalism can be described as the ability to overcome narrow mindedness and expose ourselves to new ideas, thoughts and perspectives.

A traditionally torpid and culturally colossal country with a rigid stance over modernisation which dates back to nearly a thousand years, India is a nation struggling with its own identity right now. People have adopted the contemporary outlook on liberalism but have miserably failed to incorporate it. To be liberal in India can be classified depending upon the section of the community you fit into. The orthodox of the nation see liberalism as a curse upon the youth and something that is debasing our culture while the progressive people see it as an opportunity to enjoy access to all the rights without any obligation. The main focus of liberalism is to grant every individual a sense of non-obligatory environment to live in. It lays its emphasis on personal as well as public development in socio-economic prospects.

To begin with, liberalism in India has been through a series of countless reforms. There were political reforms, social reforms, cultural reforms and economic reforms. Each and every reform led to a paradigmatic shift in the mindsets of people in a fruitful manner. Political reforms such as the inclusion of women in the Indian Parliament have stirred the cup of change. But sadly, India still ranks low (108th out of the 188 countries on the list) to have just 11 per cent female representation in the Parliament. The number of women in Parliament has shown an approximate of 20 per cent rise over the last decade compared to the number of female voters which rose from 44.3 per cent to 45.8 per cent. Voting age was reduced from 21 years to 18 years for more active participation from the youth. All these efforts were just an attempt to grant people the opportunity to exercise being liberal. They can participate in moulding the nation, according to their wants, or their needs. This by far, is the greatest asset of liberty.

Social and cultural reforms such as the Brahmo Samaj, Prarthana Samaj and the Ramakrishna Mission paved the way for abolition of petty practices such as *sati pratha*, and boldly reduced slavery, illiteracy, child marriage to a minimal. The reason behind the substantial economic development, the economic reforms such as the privatisation in the public sector, freedom to import foreign technology (under the New Industrial Policy), reduction in taxes as well as restrictions in import-export lead to increase in market desirability. To be a liberal in a nation that is going through this turmoil can be a daunting task. The growth of India ever since the end of the colonial rule has been striking. One can claim that India has risen like a phoenix from the ashes. But the reality at the ground level condones this very assertion. There has been a defined set of rules to be followed to be called a 'liberal' in India. Else, you could be mistaken for an anarchist.

The so-called liberals of the nation are concerned about the matters that are far from being called a national issue. In a nation like India where women safety is steeply following the regressive mode, there are parts of the nation where it's still considered a taboo to marry a person out of your parents' choice, doesn't having a protest over the proper choice of clothes for a celebrity or inappropriate song lyrics seems to be too ludicrous? As a result of which the liberals of the nation experience a lot of criticism from the people. It's kind of unfortunate as it makes it harder for the others, trying to promote a crucial and indispensable cause to be faced with the same kind of critique. Consequently, people look at these liberals as promoters of the western culture but not as fellow countrymen trying to bring the nation up and about in terms of liberalism.

Being liberal isn't restricted to your house, or area or your state. You have to be liberal on every perspective of a situation possible. India is nation whose land was bestowed with the toughest of the reformers, the strongest of the leaders and above all produced an articulate and one of the most intelligible constitutions in the world to rely and run its government on. Unfortunately, none of these factors are fixing the rigid outlooks of the people. It is not a rare sight to see people from the north-east treated like strangers and being called out as 'chinky'. People are treated as outsiders and are faced with the most indecent behaviour travelling from one state to another. Even after nearly 70 years of independence, it's still an ongoing debate over Islam and Christianity being foreign religions. Reservation was introduced to promote the active participation of people from the under-privileged sections of the society, which is now seen as an easy way to success by some. India is lacking a strong amendment in the law stating the caste-based reservation. The times have changed, situations have changed. Providing succour to people who deserve it should be the motto. Caste and reservation have become such imperative political agendas that political parties that divide people in the name of caste and reservation are awarded by their vote banks. The division of the nation on the basis of caste system has to be stopped, even in case of reservation. Help should be given on the basis of social and economic status, irrespective of the caste. After all, how can a country move forward when its people are competing with each other to be backward?

The world's largest democracy is facing a dilemma over being a democracy itself. On one hand where a democracy gives its people a fair chance to raise their voice, its undue advantages taken by religious extremists or opportunists can set us right aback. Indian society has its roots in our rich heritage and culture. It's about time the people realise the true meaning of liberalism. We did achieve freedom from the British 69 years ago, but are we really free?

Liberalism in India in my opinion has still not reached the corners where it desperately should. It is only a certain section of the society that is liberal that too only for selective purposes. Assaulting a couple brutally on Valentine's Day on the grounds of blasphemy does not define liberty. Curbing your daughters from going out late at night does not define liberty. Judging people on the basis of their caste also does not define liberty. Our leaders, most of all, are responsible for spreading out the right manner of exercising liberalism. Sadly, in India the story is a little different. Not even a few days had passed of the highly publicised rape case of a woman in New Delhi (nicknamed by the Indian media as "Nirbhaya" meaning "unafraid"), when exercising his right to speech the ex-Chief Minister of the Indian state of Uttar Pradesh was seen speaking in defence of the rapists on the grounds that they were merely young boys who committed a mistake for which punishment by hanging is not reasonable and is unfair. His son is serving as the current Chief Minister of the state and is no less than his father. From irresponsible handling of the communal riots that took place in Muzaffarnagar to bashing the media over critiquing his disability to manage and ensure women safety in Uttar Pradesh,

Akilesh Yadav hasn't been the role model the youth of Uttar Pradesh expected him to be.

The conservatives of the country are not just the tyrants or the orthodox; it's also our parents, relatives and could be even our friends. In India it's okay for two consenting adults to marry a stranger as long as the match is arranged by the parents, but a plight to fall in love with someone outside our caste. It's okay to blame a girl for rape because she was wearing inappropriate clothes, but so indecorous to teach a boy the proper manner of conduct with a girl. There is no doubt that Indian society had been patriarchal for as long as its traces go, but the state of women security had never been worse. Liberty, in that sense, defines itself as the freedom for women to roam the streets any time of day, in any form of clothing doing anything they want.

Another matter where young India differs significantly with the elderly is the matter of virginity. Sex is still a taboo not only in India but in South Asia. People not only look down at you if you are not celibate, but it is also frowned upon in almost all parts of the nation. It is considered immoral if you do not abstain from sex before marriage, but not a matter of concern if you produce 5 children after being wed without even the consent of the woman. In many cases if a woman becomes a widow, she is supposed to go on and spend her life as a spinster, but for a man it's absolutely essential that he doesn't end up spending his life alone. The double standards of our society are beyond understanding for people who didn't grow up here.

Liberalism in India is a misconstrued subject. It is associated with defining terrorism on the basis of religion, avenging a social mishap by damaging public property which was itself paid by our taxes, marching with a candle in hand, demanding for a caste-based reservation and then blaming the fellow countrymen for still differentiating them on the basis of caste. Hypocrisy is shining in each step of this nation in the name of liberalism. Distorting the meaning of liberalism according to oneself is also a form of liberalism. As it is said that destruction is a form of creation, it can be concluded that moulding the benefits of being liberal as per the needs of an individual is also termed as liberalism.

The country's progress is also a major virtue of the liberty promoted by the coherent and just constitution of the nation. But there is no denial that this liberalism in the hands of conservatives is devouring its ability to foster a change for greater good. It's about time that people start realising that change comes from within and it has to come now sooner than later. Raise your children in a milieu where they do not consider the opposite sex or the previously established backward castes as inferior or condescending. Raise them so that they know that all religions are equal and that being secular does not necessarily mean being anti-Hindu and being communist does not necessarily mean being anti-Muslim. Neither are all Muslims terrorists nor are all Hindus religious extremists supporting forced Hindutva. India is secular and will always be. North-east Indians are not foreigners and east-Indians are not responsible for retrograde of any state. As an Indian, you have the liberty to settle in any part of the nation without having any fear of discrimination. Use of reservation as a tool for gaining political mileage needs to be stopped. Blaming the judiciary straight up-front doesn't solve any problem. The change can only be brought by the people themselves. It has to begin from ground level; it has to begin from you.

Dole out the people who stand against it because it is our country and it is our job to make it a better place to live in. Don't let anybody tell you the limitations of your liberties. It's your choice how you use them for better or for worse.

5

CHINMAYA LAL THAKUR

Challenging Extremist Ideologies

Two specific words, 'Liberal' and 'India' form the crux of my argument in this essay. I would attempt to gloss these two words and seek to establish a link between them. This will, hopefully, be a movement towards answering the question, "What does it mean to be a Liberal in India?"

Even though there have been examples of social actions predating the enlightenment in Europe which can be labelled 'liberal' in retrospect, it is the socio-political discourse of, roughly, the 18th century that brings about a sustained focus on the philosophy that is often labelled 'liberalism'. It is important to understand that much like any other school of thought, 'liberalism' has always been marked by competing ideologies and tendencies which make it difficult for one to be precise in the delineation of its meaning. At best, one can identify broad trends and patterns in the political, economic, and social thinking that has led to the evolution of the liberal tradition. Without being pedantic about such details, in this essay, I would highlight a few aspects of the tradition of liberal philosophy and its criticisms which have a bearing on how liberalism is to be construed and understood in contemporary India.

Because liberalism relies heavily on the enlightenment discourse of the achievement of social progress through the human capacity to reason, it is not surprising that it takes the individual as its metaphysical centre. It is assumed that this individual has the power and capacity to rationally engage with socio-political concerns across space and time. The liberal subject, in this sense, is a transcendental construction. It follows therefore that liberalism, ideally, would believe that there are no limits to the human freedom to reason. It is crucial to remember in this context of the affirmation of the apparently limitless power of human cognitive reasoning that there does not seem to be a recognition of the limits of rational thinking in liberal philosophy. One only needs to recount all the excesses that have been committed on women, working classes, lower castes, and coloured races in the name of human progress and civilisation on the ostensible basis of human reason (because it is assumed that women, working classes, lower castes, and coloured races are incapable of it) to understand the implications of such thinking. This fact makes liberal philosophy rightly vulnerable to attacks from almost all the other stakeholders in the spectrum of political thinking. Marxists, feminists, and postcolonial theorists, for instance, have taken liberal philosophy to task on this account.

There is a curious paradox, however, which must be mentioned with regard to the humanist impulse in liberal thought that I have attempted to highlight in the previous paragraph. First Wave and early Second Wave feminist movements attest to the fact that the liberal impulse governed by the power of human reasoning has helped strengthen the attempt to establish a certain gendered social equity and inclusivity. Even as one would rightly argue that underlying this equity and inclusivity is the paternalistic impulse inherent to liberal humanism, it cannot be denied that consequent thinking about issues related to politics of identity and resistance would perhaps have been difficult without this impulse in liberal thought to grant the fact that, at least theoretically, all human beings are equal and have the right to work towards their own socio-political and economic advancement. Unsurprisingly, the consequence of this paradox has been another rather well-argued critique of liberalism which seeks to radically sharpen its political tooth. Contra the historical experience of the French Revolution which, in a sense, was the real political manifestation of the liberal thought of the philosophes such as Voltaire, Rousseau, and Diderot, it is now argued that there is a wider divide between liberal espousals of the principles of equality and freedom and the social movements that actually lead to some progress towards these ideals.

It is in the above related context of the twin attack on the tradition of Western liberal philosophy—one forcefully highlighting the limits of rational thinking and the other underlining the 'fence sitting' that seems to have engulfed liberal politics—that I wish to contextualise liberalism with regard to contemporary India. To be a liberal in today's India means to be critically conscious of and not succumb to several extremist social pressures and ideologies. This understanding of liberalism, as I hope to demonstrate in the rest of this essay, does not necessarily need an endeavour to go beyond the various models and principles that Indian liberalism has adopted and adapted from the European tradition. In other words, I seek to argue that to be a liberal in India means to be able to resist and challenge extremist ideologies without sacrificing a critical attitude towards the principles that often guide this very challenge.

The 'Idea of India', a phrase repeated ad nauseam since the publication of Sunil Khilnani's *The Idea of India* (1997), rightly evokes an inclusive vision of post-Independence India that is reflected in the deliberations that have led to the writing of the Constitution. Nehru has come to be the representative of this tradition that believes in the simultaneous celebration of the socio-political diversity that marks Indian society and Parliamentary democracy as the expression of the collective political will of India's citizens. An Indian liberal cannot but identify with this sentiment of understanding of the social as a shared space which is marked by the presence of various stakeholders of multiple socio-political views. Any threat to the idea of India, therefore, is a threat to a liberal conception of India that recognises India's diversity and democracy as its strengths.

A liberal in India today is critically conscious of a twin attack on India's diversity from the opposing poles of the political spectrum. Extemism, the liberal realises, seeks to take advantage of the socio-economic disparities that exist in a society. Leftist extremism in the form of Maoism, for instance, has engulfed several parts of the country, particularly its central and eastern regions. Because Maoism believes in violence to achieve the ostensible aim of social transformation, it belies a lack of faith in the will of the people of India as it is expressed in the form of Parliamentary democracy and an adherence to the principles propounded in the Constitution. Similarly disconcerting is the exclusivist nature of a certain kind of

Rightist thinking that deliberately excludes some sections of India's society, particularly its religious minorities, from its imagination of India. This has been reflected in the way in which the freedom of expression of writers such as Wendy Doniger has been curtailed, the importance of national institutions such as the Indian Council for Historical Research and the Film and Television Institute of India have been subverted, and more frighteningly, the ambit of individual freedom has been narrowed by seeking to restrict the right to privacy and choice of lifestyle as reflected in matters of food, dressing etc.

Unsurprisingly, a critical consciousness of the existence and workings of these social pressures on the part of the Indian liberal is not sufficient. The need of the hour requires an active espousal of principles that form the heart of liberal thinking about the simultaneous coexistence of opposing beliefs in a society that gives equal opportunity for all such beliefs to be held and expressed. Sadly, Indian liberals seem to have fallen short in this endeavour. With regard to the judgement of the Supreme Court recognising homosexuality as a criminal act, for instance, it needed to be recognised and expressed by the Indian liberals that the judgement goes against the basic premise of 'tolerance' that has been central to the Western liberal tradition as reflected in the works of John Stuart Mill and John Rawls, and the Indian adaptations (in Gandhi and Nehru) of it. Recognising the right of people to choose and express their sexual identity should have reflected the fact that liberalism strongly calls for the tolerance of alternate socio-political views even if they might be contrary to what is the conventional and/or popular belief.

Thus, it seems to me, that to be a liberal in India today is to be a 'critical insider'. I draw this felicitous turn of phrase from one of the strongest proponents of Indian liberalism, the Kannada writer U.R. Ananthamurthy. By this, I mean that an Indian liberal needs to be critical of his/her own liberal tradition from the 'inside' while using concepts and principles from this very tradition to challenge extremist and exclusivist ideologies in the 'outside'.

6

DIWAKAR SHARMA

Liberty, Democracy and Rights

As one of the basic tenets of the French revolution, the ideal of liberty has become the foundation of modern society. Liberalism as a political ideology has held its ground since the 18th century. However the term 'liberty' has been in use since the 14th century. As the feudal system in the West broke down and capitalism created a new middle class which depended on trade and profits, liberalism found popular support, inspired masses called for abolition of monarchy, absolutism, authority of church and the landed aristocracy. They were against the unfair idea of privileges by virtue of birth. The revolutionary appeal was too strong to resist and people across the continents were inspired, leading to democratic revolutions in England, France and North America. Entrenched in reason, enlightenment and Kantian ethics, liberalism became the dominant ideology of the democratic West so much so that it gradually became a taboo to question its principles.

In spite of its success, it is really hard to form any consensus on the meaning of liberty. It is synonymous with 'freedom'. Freedom is generally defined as the absence of constraints in the exercise of an individual's rights. Although liberals concede that some external constraints are required in order to avoid chaos in society, there are certain basic moral rights which must be made available to a person in order to let her achieve self-actualisation. Locke believed in natural rights which he identified as 'life, liberty and property'. For Thomas Jefferson, they were 'life, liberty and pursuit of happiness'. Classical liberalism propounded 'negative liberty' by restricting the state's ability to interfere in one's life. On the other hand, modern liberalism suggests 'positive liberty' i.e., freedom from the social and economic conditions that hinder an individual's progress. A modern liberal believes there is a role to be played by the welfare state.

Hence even in the West, the notion of liberty has been changing. Faced by the problems thrown up by increasing industrialisation and challenge from Marxism, liberalism reinvented itself in 19th and 20th century. It lost its revolutionary zeal and became increasingly conservative as the status quo was that of liberalism.

In India, the term closest to 'liberty' is '*mukti*'. However, this term has spiritual and other-worldly connotation. With the introduction of Western education in India by the British and English as medium of instruction, the ideals prevalent in the West, such as liberty, were also imbibed by many young, upper class Indians in 19th century. The pioneer of Indian enlightenment is believed to be Raja Ram Mohan Roy, a great liberal. He was an internationalist, a scholar and reformist. The Indian society of the time had become decadent, ridden with caste-based inequalities as well as superstitions. He took it upon himself to free those who face such inequalities and reform the society. It was due to his efforts that '*sati*', a cruel practice in which the widow is burnt alive, was abolished by the British Governor General, Lord Bentinck. He established 'Brahmo Samaj', an organisation dedicated to work against superstitious, unreasonable beliefs and social inequalities. Like Brahmo Samaj, many such organisations questioned the authority of priests. One of the most important contributions of such organisations was that they translated the scriptures into regional languages so that ordinary people could read and understand them themselves. Raja Ram Mohan Roy himself was a scholar of many languages.

Early liberals like Raja Ram Mohan Roy, Derozio, Ishwar Chandra Vidyasagar and others laid the important foundation of the modern Indian society on which the Indian national movement was to be built. The Indian national movement had numerous outstanding figures all of whom held the idea of liberty dear. For some, liberty meant just political liberty i.e., self-rule. For some others like Netaji Subhas Chandra Bose, Pandit Jawaharlal Nehru and Dr B.R. Ambedkar, it included socio-economic liberty. They were of the view that political liberty or freedom from colonial rule is of no consequence unless the emancipation of masses burdened by social and economic hardships, takes place.

Amid all this, it was Mahatma Gandhi who gave a novel and the most comprehensive understanding of the term 'liberty'. Gandhi called liberty '*Swaraj*' and his idea was rooted in ancient Hindu philosophy as much as the modern Western philosophy. To him, *Swaraj* implied both outward as well as inward freedom. Outward freedom included political, social and economic freedom, whereas inward freedom refers to spiritual freedom. He urged his followers to be free from ignorance, hatred, intolerance and greed because these impede a person's path to self-realisation or '*moksha*'. In other words, *Swaraj* means complete rule over oneself, internally as well as externally.

It was this idea of *Swaraj* that motivated Gandhi to fight tooth and nail against British oppressive rule on the one hand while continuously fighting against the injustices in the society on the other. He worked among the masses, going to villages working for the betterment of the rural people including the untouchables. He called untouchables '*Harijan*' or God's people. His call to action would bring all people from diverse backgrounds to the fore. Throughout his struggle, he tried to bring Hindus and Muslims together while the British were clearly pursuing the policy of 'divide and rule'. His calls to non-violence, unity, fasts and prayers somehow brought peace to the eastern state of Bengal which was partitioned by the British in 1947 and where Hindus and Muslims were on a violent spree, killing each other for vengeance.

Hence, we see that the ideal of liberty has influenced Indians since long and was known to them in its modern sense as soon as it became a powerful force in the West. Indian nationalists had deep interest in global affairs at all times and respected the democratic and liberal ideals of the West. It may not be wrong to say that Mahatma Gandhi expanded the meaning of liberty and gave it a spiritual dimension. This is one of his many contributions to politics and philosophy. It feels humbling to inherit such legacies.

The idea of India as a nation was like a big experiment of organising a number of societies quite different from each other.

It may not be wrong to say that it was the biggest such experiment since the idea of federal structure of the USA. Post-independence, India naturally adopted a liberal and democratic polity, inspired by the ideals of its freedom struggle. The Preamble of the Indian Constitution reaffirms this. The Constitution of India is a highly progressive one. It guarantees universal adult suffrage which was quite radical at the time of its adoption when around 80 per cent population was illiterate. Also, the diversity of beliefs, aftermath of partition etc., were certain other factors that threatened to make the experiment of democratic India turn out to be a failure. However, this has not happened and India emerged as a healthy democracy. Every Indian citizen is guaranteed certain Fundamental Rights by the Constitution. Article 19 contains the list of five rights contained in Right to Freedom. These include the right to freedom of speech and expression, the right to assemble peaceably, the right to move freely etc. Article 21 is the "Right to life and personal liberty". Over the years, the Supreme Court of India has given a very broad meaning to this article. On the social front, it abolished untouchability and gave reservations in legislatures to scheduled castes (untouchables) and scheduled tribes. To provide backward classes economic liberty, the Indian Constitution guarantees reservation in public jobs and educational institutions. At the same time, the government runs a huge welfare system to support the poor, backward and other disadvantaged groups. This ensures that they are liberated in the true sense of the word.

While many other developing countries accepted liberal democracy on their independence, they quickly went back to civil wars, totalitarianism, etc., due to the absence of industrialisation, capitalism, and their political environment. On the other hand, India remains the largest liberal democratic nation in the world even though India was not industrialised at the time of independence and was in fact the poorest in the world. In my opinion, the strong values inherited by Indians from the freedom struggle are responsible for this.

After Independence, India decided to go for a planned economy in order to achieve industrialisation as quickly as possible. Along the way, the Indian political and economic system became more and more centralised. This resulted in lower growth rate. However, the disintegration of the Soviet Union in 1991 resulted in the decline in the appeal of centralised socialism all over the world. India was also not unaffected by this. Hence, it is not a surprise that LPG (liberalisation, privatisation and globalisation) came to India in the same year. Post economic reforms, India has posted high growth rates consistently. Currently, India is a 2 trillion USD economy having a higher growth rate than China. Trade to and from India is increasing each year and Indian businesses have emerged as global leaders. The new government in Delhi appears to be tending towards neoliberalism in the sense that it believes in minimal hindrances to businesses, abolition of 'red-tapism' and transparency in government functioning.

India is composed of quite a diverse set of communities, each having their own customs and beliefs. The 21st century India is quite a vibrant society to live in. Ancient traditions and beliefs are being put to question almost every day. There are a number of factors for this. Obviously the political environment, with its multi-party democracy system, is available. Then there is an increase in the number of educated people. Literacy has now reached around 74 per cent. Increased women workforce participation, a large number of youth, increased incomes, Internet as a fast way of communication etc., are challenging the fabric of society.

As a young Indian, I find it quite amazing that my generation is ready to accept changes at some level, something that was taboo during my parents' times. The fast pace of changes is sometimes harrowing for my parents. But even they are ready to accept a revision in our belief systems. For me and many other urban Indians, social media is a medium that we use to express our views and come to know about others'. It is quite common to find outpourings on social media against any unfair government action. So much so that many times the government has had to take its steps back. This is quite exciting for me as I feel that I can also influence decision-making. Maybe this is how a true democracy should be.

The recent trial of a terror convict Yakub Memon is a case in point. It was surprising to find so many people on social media petitioning against giving the convict the death penalty. While I don't deny that there was no consensus and maybe the majority was against showing any mercy, it was quite heartening to see that many were questioning the need for such drastic measure undertaken in the name of checking the growth of terrorism when the empirical data is against this.

While radicalism and religious fundamentalism are having sway over a major part of the world, an average Indian is increasingly becoming more tolerant of others' views and beliefs. This is due to changed priorities in today's times. Many Indians now don't give that much importance to religion. This clearly shows the effects of capitalism on Indian society. Today's youth work in MNCs, consume global products and services, and may have to work anywhere in India or even abroad. In a way, actual integration is happening now.

However, there is a lot India and Indians need to do in order to become a true 'liberal' country. There is no doubt that economic policies are going to become more and more amenable to trade and business. However, there are still many areas in the society which are a taboo for a liberal. For example, homosexuality is still illegal according to the Supreme Court even though it has recognised transgender as a third gender. Women empowerment is another area which requires more attention. Even though women enrolment in schools is increasing, the patriarchal mindset of some Indians is hindering the process. Many atrocities are committed to subjugate them. Women's participation in legislatures is also low. Women find it hard to find jobs and manage work and household. Similarly, the condition of backward classes and tribals has not improved even after 68 years of independence. Many still face discrimination and don't have access to basic amenities. While liberalism is increasingly influencing the urban people, the rural masses have not been integrated into the national debate. Many social prejudices still exist there. This is due to low literacy, and lack of other basic facilities in rural areas.

Then there is the challenge of religious fundamentalism. There are some people who claim that ours is an ancient civilization and the tradition that we have inherited is sacrament. Contemporary politics show the prevalence of such issues in national debates. While an Indian liberal holds dear the value of secularism enshrined in the Constitution, it is constantly under fire of certain intolerant elements who want to divide the society along communal lines.

So, while the idea of liberty has come a long way in India, it still has to go far. Any compromise on the ideals of liberty, democracy and rights, will be a betrayal of the efforts and sacrifices made by our ancestors who were involved in the Indian national movement.

7

HARISH ALAGAPPA

The Decline and Fall of Indian Liberalism

The existence of the modern democratic republic India owes a deep debt to the philosophy of liberalism. Indian thinkers from Raja Ram Mohan Roy all the way to Jawaharlal Nehru were heavily influenced by Western ideas of uninfringeable freedoms as a birth right of every man and woman, and used them as the foundation to effect at first social, and later, political change across the country. However, the last few years have seen a marked shift in the direction of popular Indian thought; it is not so much a departure as a complete repudiation of the ideals on which modern India was founded. Liberalism's position as the foundation of modern Indian thought is slowly being replaced by a resurgent right-wing conservative ideology that espouses as its core tenets, the rejection of any and all liberal ideas and a fervent adherence to a dogma centred on hero-worshipping an imagined past in an effort to facilitate the imposition of social, and in some cases political, boundaries that the founders of the Indian independence movement aimed to eliminate. Indeed, if election results can be taken to be an accurate reflection of the ideological zeitgeist, liberals appear to be dwindling in number, or at least are now less in the limelight or in positions of power as radical conservatives.

Of course, the conservative-liberal divide is a feature of all modern democracies, although those terms were rarely invoked in the Indian context until recently. The source of the divide, in India at least, can be traced to the effects of the application of liberal ideology on existing social and political constructs and the demolition of power structures that had otherwise held sway across the subcontinent for centuries. It is thus no surprise the earliest and most vocal opponents of liberalism in India were the religious elite.

The caste system, a mainstay of the Indian social landscape for nearly 3,000 years, is threatened by liberal statements about the equality of all people. As all major religions are profoundly patriarchal, they find themselves further in opposition to liberal demands for women to be treated the same as men in all spheres of life. And fundamentalists of all major denominations are so opposed to the idea of freedom of religion that they have started to use the word 'secular' as an insult directed at their liberal opponents.

Liberalism advocates certain freedoms, later enshrined in the Indian Constitution as fundamental rights, which are seen by people in privileged or elite positions in society as a threat to their place on the totem place, a location that they perceive to be almost a part of the natural order of things. This desire amongst certain groups or individuals to maintain the status quo, or more insidiously, to limit the transfer of opportunities that they already possess to individuals or people who they have historically treated as inferior, is at the core of all opposition to liberal ideology, either overtly or so subliminally that anti-liberals are unaware of the presence of these ingrained biases.

Indian liberals, of course, are not entirely without blame. If vast swathes of the Indian populace have been driven away from liberalism and found comfort in the familiar yet proto-fascist philosophies espoused by right-wing conservatives of all creeds and castes, it is not so much a failure of Indian liberalism as it is a failure of Indian liberals.

In the decades immediately following Independence, India embarked on a long, torrid, and ultimately fruitless love affair with Fabian socialism, exemplified by Jawaharlal Nehru's unwavering trust in the principles of the philosophy, which he was indoctrinated into at a young age through family friend Annie Besant, and later studied extensively during his days at Trinity College, Cambridge, and the Inns of Court School of Law in London. In his autobiography, Nehru described Fabian socialism as: "not merely an economic doctrine which I favour" but "(...) a vital creed which I hold with all my head and heart." The unquestioning acceptance of this Statist doctrine was a hallmark of early post-Independence India, but underneath the veneer of what looked like classic left-liberalism, Nehru's ideological approach revealed a far less altruistic view of the common man.

One of the foundations of any liberal philosophy is the understanding that all men and women are created equal and are not only capable of, but deserve, the opportunity to be in control of their own destinies. Life, liberty, and the pursuit of happiness are interlinked goals, for one should have the liberty to pursue their happiness. Nehru's Fabian society did not think the majority of the Indian population was capable of this pursuing their own path to happiness, particularly in the arena of commerce. His vision of India was a sort of nanny economy, where the government was essentially responsible for almost every aspect of the production and distribution of goods and services. In 1951, India had a literacy rate of 18.33 per cent; it was due to this lack of education that early Indian socialists felt the average Indian citizen was incapable of taking rational decisions critical to their well-being and happiness, save that of voting during elections. Thus, for the first 40-odd years of independent India, liberalism existed merely in its social form; economic liberalism was seen as a too dangerous idea to be left in the hands of a largely uneducated populace. Consequently, wealth and power remained concentrated in the hands of India's educated elites, people who had ironically been ingrained with the ideas of social liberalism. And, thus, was born perhaps the single most hypocritical entity known to humankind, a creature known as the Lutyens Delhi Liberal.

Named after the extremely wealthy and exclusive neighbourhoods of central Delhi, designed by Edwin Lutyens between 1912 and 1930, the Lutyens Delhi Liberal is and needs to remain a democracy while conveniently ignoring the modern day feudalistic social and economic practices that have brought them to a position of such privilege. They speak eloquently of liberal ideas of fundamental freedoms and the equality of all people while living in bungalows on tree-lined avenues replete with a retinue of underpaid and overworked maids, servants, and drivers who cater to their every whim. For a long time, the Lutyens Delhi Liberal was representative of Indian liberalism, and thus also represented the mistakes that had occurred during the process of transmutation of classical liberalism into an Indian context.

In order to understand the oddly oxymoronic juxtapositions of philosophies that have led to the great ideological divide present in modern India at the moment, we have to look at perhaps the single most important event in post-Independence Indian history; the economic liberalisation of the India in the early 1990s. Following the gradual opening up of the restrictive and inward-looking Indian economy, we saw the rapid rise of the Indian middle class. The Nehruvian Fabian Socialist Liberal was seen by many members of the now powerful Indian middle class as the reason why it took them so long to be able to ascend the socio-economic ladder. Thus, to many middle-class Indians raised in a post-liberalisation economy, social liberalism was seen as the ideology of the wealthy dilettante, which possibly explains why so many of them, on reaching adulthood, were taken in by and voted for the opposite worldview during the 2014 General Elections.

Indian liberals have not taken this defeat well. Rather than introspect on the failings in their ideology and approach that led to this defeat, they have instead decided to either wallow in their own victimhood or try and make peace with the new bosses as best they can. This action too will earn them no sympathy from the opposite side, as it reveals the same elitism that caused their downfall. Rather than explore the reasons for the other side's success, the immediate aftermath of the 2014 elections saw Indian liberals accusing right-wingers of manipulating innocent, which is a subtle way of saying simple-minded, voters or of revealing a large proportion of the Indian population to be inherently bloodthirsty degenerates. The high-handed moralising of Indian liberals have not gone down well with conservatives and any attempts by the former to reach out across the divide have featured such staggering amounts of smug, self-reverential pride that it comes as no surprise when the latter refuse to accept any token of friendship.

Indian liberals need to see the flaws in their interpretation of classical liberalism, the first and foremost one being their inability to see their opponents as equals. Preaching about the equality of all individuals is easy enough and Indian liberals never tire of speaking about how they acknowledge first and foremost that all individuals; man or woman, LGBT or straight, high caste or low caste, rich or poor are born equal. Yet, they consistently refuse to acknowledge that a conservative viewpoint could be valid when seen from the point of view of the opposite side. Equality has never been an easy idea for us Indians to digest, we are too used to hierarchies and it takes a concentrated amount of effort to ever truly see people from a lower station of society as our equals, all while clamouring for our superiors to acknowledge us as their equals.

Of course, one may ask the very valid question of why I am advocating a one-way exchange; why are people on the right not expected to see the world from our viewpoint, why must it always be the responsibility of the liberal to seek out and understand his or her opponent. The answer to that is simple. Because that's what liberals do. Liberalism is a philosophy that is built on the foundation of two words, freedom and equality. This implies understanding that all individuals are equal and are free to follow the diktats of their conscience, though obviously not without consequence. Thus, acknowledging the conservative worldview as something formulated by people who are our equals and giving them the freedom to espouse it is the very essence of liberal thought. Right-wing ideology is built on the foundation that the opposite is wrong no matter what. I am not advocating token lip service to an ideology that's currently in power, rather I would say being an Indian liberal involves gathering as comprehensive an understanding of various viewpoints as is possible. It is not necessary to agree with them or like them or even tolerate them. You are free to call out racism, sexism, and xenophobia for being the hate-filled excuses of a delusional worldview they are, but by understanding where the hate comes from, it becomes possible to try and prevent it from growing, spreading, and infecting more people.

Right-wing fundamentalism is an unsustainable, untenable philosophy. It aims to maintain the status quo in a universe where the only constant is change. The sudden popularity of right-wing fundamentalism among a target market one rarely sees forming the core of a right-wing movement, *viz.*, young, educated, middle class individuals, is a reaction to the exclusivity and elitism that Indian liberalism has portrayed. For all its talk of equality and freedom, young Indians felt alienated and frustrated by Indian liberalism, it was believed that Indian liberals were modern-day aristocrats who simply spoke in sophisticated, high-handed rhetoric. By humbling itself, Indian liberalism will find that many of their opponents in fact share many of their concerns, ideas, and approaches to life.

Indian liberalism, as it has existed for the last half century, is an ideology that was tried and has failed spectacularly. It must be replaced with a philosophy that eschews the moral high ground that liberals seem to think is their exclusive property and instead cultivate the ability to see themselves, and the world, from the eyes of their enemy, and acknowledge the view as something that was formulated by an equal. Any man or woman who can accomplish this would be a true Indian liberal.

8

REIJUL SACHDEV

The Great Indian Circus Free-k Show!

In the *Ballad of Reading Gaol*, Oscar Wilde claims, "We know not whether laws be right/Or whether laws be wrong/All we know that lie in gaol/Is that the walls are strong." But to be a liberal in India is to look beyond the walls of tradition and conservatism and ask not just whether the laws are right, but whether the walls need be there at all.

Say the word 'liberal' in India and (more often than not) you are immediately associated with feminism, Greenpeace, Maoists, Arvind Kejriwal, being a bleeding heart and other 'disruptive influences'. But, to me, being a liberal in India is simply about respecting and cherishing freedom. It means recognising freedom as an aspect of sentient life itself and not as a commodity to be handed out to the most deserving.

For me, an important aspect of liberalism is tolerance. Being a liberal means being willing to embrace and accept the existence of differences. In India, people tend to have multiple identities—on the basis of religion, economic status, place of birth, educational qualifications, caste, gender, etc. This multiplicity of identities leads to a whole host of differences. A liberal in India has the unenviable task of recognising people for the men (and women) behind these identity masks.

In a country where individual identities are usually caught up with cultural and family identities, being a liberal does not mean ignoring all masks and trying to make society follow suit. Instead, it is about recognising the mask for what it is and not mistaking it for the face. For example, most Indian parents encourage their children to study either engineering or medicine at an undergraduate level. Liberal parents ought not to completely ignore the presence of various social pressures for studying different subjects, but to respect the child's decision after informing him/her of the social context.

In this way, a liberal also loses access to different sects of society. In fact, being a liberal can sometimes feel like being a pariah! But yet, in a sense, liberalism in India is also a deeply unifying notion. While it may not help you connect with specific people based on social labels, it does help you connect with people as a whole based on a concept which many tend to forget—the concept of India.

India is a melting pot of cultures, faiths and languages. Politically, separatist tendencies have been witnessed in many areas, like the Maoist-tribal insurgencies in Chhattisgarh and the separatist movement in Kashmir. States have clashed over issues like water usage (e.g. the Karnataka-Tamil Nadu dispute over the Cauvery river). States have also been partitioned because of strong differences and political agitations, as in the case of Andhra Pradesh and Telengana. Economically, the disparity remains so high that any self-respecting Marxist would conclude that a labour revolution is imminent. According to the Indian Human Development Survey (2004-05), the top 1 per cent earns over 8 times what half the population earns in a month! Culturally, there still exist concepts like '*gotra*' (a kind of sub-caste) which divides people to such an extent that intra-*gotra* marriages can lead to murder. These divisions run deep and tend to fragment society. It is only from the resin of liberalism that the glue called India can be manufactured.

This is not to say that every liberal must be a jingoistic self-proclaimed patriot, spreading the message of Indian unity. Rather, just by respecting other's freedoms liberals naturally help unite people without engendering feelings of hostility as a totalitarian repressive regime might. In fact, an important part of liberalism is also accepting (though not necessarily agreeing with!) criticisms of the nation, its policies and people.

While the task of a liberal so far seems insurmountable, the reality is not so bleak. In a country with over a billion people, where one meets a new face almost everyday, one can hardly be blamed for making generalisations (using social identities) in order to cope with interactions on such a large scale. Further, while people do divide society based on their distinct identities, Indians are almost always united in defending their freedoms—be it from the British Raj or Indira Gandhi's Emergency. The danger lies in groups of like-minded individuals trying to preserve their freedoms and identities to the exclusion of all others.

For we are all united by our love of liberty, but as Oscar Wilde puts it: "Each man kills the thing he loves." Thus, when one group becomes fanatic about defending its freedoms, this leads to a state of fear—fear of the indefinable alien 'other'. When this fear manifests itself (via laws, economic sanctions, etc.), this marks the onset of orthodoxy and eventually leads to a conservative mindset, unwilling to accept differences. The irony is that in trying to protect our freedoms, we kill the liberal attitude from which they originate. Of course, this fine line between protecting one's own freedom while also respecting the freedoms of others is one which every liberal must walk. However, in India, the problem is compounded by the fact that there are so many people each of whom expects different freedoms based on his/her various identities. Further, many of these expectations are rooted in traditions of intolerance, (e.g., the idea of caste) further complicating the issue.

A case in point is the system of caste-based reservations for Other Backward Castes (OBCs) in higher educational institutions. In striving to protect the interests of the oppressed, the Government has caused a resulting increase in tensions between OBCs and regular students at colleges. This is not to say that reservations are a bad idea per se or that preserving the status quo is ideal. But economic reservations might be more useful in this context, as they would prevent the 'creamylayer' of OBCs (who have long overcome their humble origins and are now relatively well-positioned in society) from unfairly exploiting the system.

Note that this fear of the 'other' occurs not only among minorities or marginalised social groups, but (arguably more frequently) also in the majority. This is especially dangerous in a democratic set-up if the majority become oppressors of other groups. For example, the incorporation of Hindu mythological ideas into school history text books stems from an innate desire to protect one's beliefs.

Unfortunately, in this case, it was carried a little too far, as later admitted by NCERT (National Council for Educational Research and Training) itself.

Similar fears are also observed in both economic and social contexts. For example, the condemnation of Greenpeace and its activities by firms like Essar (and even the Government itself!) and the suspension of its funds stems again from a desire to protect the current economic status quo.

Yet, strangely, though our group-based identities make us less liberal on a small scale, they also make our society more liberal as a whole. Though Indians might seem less liberal at an individual level, by protecting the freedoms and balancing the interests of various groups, society as a whole remains liberal in its outlook. For instance, the large number of political parties and stand points in India leads to a form of coalition politics which makes it harder for anyone party to unilaterally impose its views on the nation. Similarly, peaceful protests like the Chipko (for stopping deforestation) and the Lokpal (for battling corruption) movements have helped balance the interests of various groups so that eventual compromises are reached while respecting as many freedoms as possible.

Some might call a set-up like this anarchy, but, in truth, it is no more anarchy than a direct democracy. The idea is not that one guiding group should have sufficient social power to impose its will on the others. Instead, each group should have its own freedoms respected while respecting the freedoms of others. This gives society a framework for expanding in which ever direction people choose. Finally, if a particular social direction is really the will of most people, then that direction will eventually be taken by various groups unifying, e.g. the conviction of Manu Sharma in the Jessica Lal murder case, despite his father's (Vinod Sharma) political influence. To me, this is one of the most important aspects of being a liberal in India—keeping the bridges open so that groups can fragment as well as unify. By allowing people to move freely between these liberal groups, we are essentially maintaining individual freedoms as well.

In this respect, an important role is played by the judiciary. In India, the judicial system is responsible for safeguarding the freedoms allotted by the legislatures. The Supreme Court also has the power to declare any law '*ultra vires*' and against the letter and/or spirit of the Constitution. The judiciary is thus essential for liberal principles. For example, the Allahabad High Court has helped to settle the Ayodhya dispute—a bone of contention for both Hindus and Muslims (both of whom believed the land to be sacred and their exclusive right). The High Court split the land, thereby preserving as much religious freedom as possible.

Similarly, the Supreme Court scrapped 214 out of 218 coal blocks allocated by the Government since 1993 to balance principles of social justice with economic development. It is clear that for any Indian liberal, the judiciary can be a potent weapon.

However, a major problem of the Indian judiciary is the huge delay most cases experience. For example, the Ayodhya dispute was resolved only after a period of 60 years! This arises from the vast backlog of cases. In 2014, there were over 30 million court cases pending judgement! While some might think this makes India's judiciary non-functional, in truth it creates a dynamic equilibrium with legal interpretive flexibility available to all parties. This might sound like a bad thing, but it is essential for liberalism's survival.

This flexibility enables a liberal to oppose certain laws. For example, Section 377 of the Indian Penal Code recognises homosexuality as a criminal offence. The Supreme Court chose to uphold this law in 2013. The move was widely condemned by liberals, but what could they do? While campaigning for the legal amendments, should they bow to a discriminatory law? If Gandhi had never violated any law, India might still be a colony today. I think a liberal has a duty to balance the Rule of Law with one's freedom from oppression. When certain laws restrict individual freedoms without increasing society's freedom as a whole, I think that marks a clash with liberalism. In these situations, I think the low throughput rate of the courts can help liberals to interpret the law in line with liberal ideas, without coming into direct conflict with the law. For example, many turn a blind eye to homosexual activities and do not report them, forming an independent equilibrium, without clashing with the courts. A liberal needs to walk this fine line between anarchy and tyranny—guided by the principle of jointly maximising individual and collective social freedoms.

This does not in any way mean that a liberal should flout judicial verdicts or that liberalism implies not punishing the guilty. In fact, liberals ought to support just punishment as per the law, e.g. the hanging of the rapists in the Nirbhaya case after nationwide public outcries.

However, trying to assassinate the rapists in the name of liberalism is clearly absurd. Public opinion can thus act as a tool for speeding up police investigations, arrests, etc, as in the Nirbhaya case. The courts then deliver the judgements after suitable deliberation. This way society protects its freedoms. But by respecting the authority of the courts and the police, we prevent mob rule and respect the freedoms of individuals as well. Thus, justice can be meted out swiftly and judgements delivered thoughtfully. To me, being a liberal is about interpreting the law to balance mob justice with the Rule of Law.

Finally, we come to the medium of liberalism—expression and its freedom. In India, the large number of groups means that offending sensibilities seems very easy—as the British found out during the Revolt of 1857 and Shashi Tharoor found out during his (in)famous "cattle class" tweet controversy in 2009! Further more, a lot of intra-group remarks and conversations are aimed at inciting feelings of resentment or condescension towards members of some other group, e.g. parochial sentiments expressed by regional political parties like the Shiv Sena in Maharashtra. Surely some limits are needed to the freedom of expression. Even in the US, the recent controversy over President Obama's use of the N-word displays the fact that such limits exist. How then does a liberal draw the line between freedom from abuse and freedom to express?

I think that a liberal approach here involves allowing for the segmentation of public broadcast channels, in much the same way that groups arise based on differences in beliefs and ideologies. Be it TV airtime or web forums, by explicitly advertising the type of views they wish to express, they can allow people to either view or discard the opinions expressed.

Groups of people will then naturally associate with the type of content they can relate to. Of course, as Arnab Goswami (the well-know TV anchor of the nightly Newshour debates on Times Now) might point out, "The nation has a right to know!" and news channels, newspapers, etc. ought to report all manner of content. This could, of course, colour people's perceptions, but by strengthening libel and slander laws and making litigation more accessible such issues could be overcome.

This contrasts sharply with the unilateral approach taken by the Maharashtra government towards the All India Bakchod Roast (of Arjun Kapoor and Raanveer Singh) video uploaded on YouTube. In response to a complaint filed about the video being offensive, the government launched a probe into AIB, till the video was finally removed from YouTube.

Funnily enough (pun intended!), humour has long been a thorny issue for Indian society. Indians tend to enjoy laughing at others (reducing the fear of the 'other'), while having a hard time laughing at themselves. For me, the liberal approach here involves accepting the existence of humour in all its varied forms. Just as North Indians joke about how South Indians nod their heads, so too do South Indians joke about the aggressiveness of North Indians. Being a liberal in India means being able to laugh at (or at least not get readily offended by) both types of jokes.

In conclusion, being a liberal in India is a balancing act. It's about balancing tradition with freedom, one group with an other and wit with retort. But most of all, it's about being open-minded and imaginative enough to see someone else's perspective, as well as to not take oneself too seriously, for as Francis Bacon put it: "Imagination was given to man to compensate him for what he is not; a sense of humour to console him for what he is".

9

HARSHITA LALL

The Liberating Phoenix

Across the waters, up to the far tides, where the horizon kissed the foaming skin of the sea, the sunlight escaped. It spread its tendrils over the vastly curling waves, their mouths opening to swallow each other like a predator chasing a young foal to swallow it whole. The tide washed at my feet, leaving its foaming remains to touch them as the sweeping sunlight blanketed it with fading warmth.

I am Indian. I am a Woman. I am not free.

It was there, where the sea met the horizon, that I saw you. You were like a Goddess, enveloped in the density of the waves, your hair tumbling down as they caressed your slightly curved shoulders. Your lips laughed the gleam of the shy sunlight and your teeth shone like the pearls gifted by the sea that enveloped you.

I strongly believe in democracy. I am a citizen of the largest democracy in the world. I am a 'liberal'. I believe in personal freedom. I am not a 'liberal'. I do not have personal freedom.

You looked at me from the distance, your eyes emitted the glow of your soul, shinning pure gold. You smiled and it seemed as though the whole sea was laughing, its frothing dances your reverential celebration.

You were the beauty of the stars; you were the glow in a mother's heart when she first looks at her newborn, you were the sensation on one's neck when the wind blows, gently caressing it; you were the love in a man's heart for the woman who would not love him back.

Where, then, is personal liberty? The 'you' who sets impossible standards, demands infinitely and mocks on my plainness? Or the 'I' who is the young Indian still waiting to gain freedom after 68 years of Independence?

What would I give to have you—consume you, fuse with you. Your very essence seemed to be calling out to me, the tilt of your head beckoning at my feet.

I was drunk in you. Your arched neck, your glittering eyes. Your skin gleaming on your arched waist as you twist in grace. I look at you, and then I look at me. I am the essence of your repulsion. I am twisted. I am short. The darkness of my skin hides the treacherous fat of my shapeless body. I stand in the shade, an ugly representation of each person's worst fear.

How can I aspire for freedom when I am made to feel inferior every day? If everything is bigger than me: The 'you' that is the Government whose twisted power lies in its intense hold over every 'I'? The Government kills every 'I' slowly and steadily each day, with corruption and cunningness, bribery and buffoonery.

I am the cog in the wheel that makes 'you' beautiful. You, India, are the annihilating, immense power that takes away my liberty. I live every day as a young Indian woman—trapped, cracking and scared, still daring to aspire personal liberty, shouting slogans knowing your shapely ears will not listen to my screams, crying tears that you will consider dirt as endless crimes are heaped upon my person, and yet, fighting forward.

What I would give to be you—to have your beauty, to walk your grace. I spent a lifetime trying to hide my plainness, attempting to subside the extent of my worthlessness in a material world.

I walk closer and closer towards you. Your beauty hurts my eyes. My chafing skin feels trapped in the power of your grace. If I were you, I would have the boy who spurned me, the friends who I dreamed of, the confidence that remained knotted at the pit of my stomach.

I know I am tiny as compared to your vastness, I know I am incomparable to you, India, but I want to be you. I want to be free like you, democratic like you, 'liberal', like you. I want to be undistorted and undeniable like you, a superpower and the leader of the future like you. I want New India to have a Pillar of Liberty and not just imitate the land of The Statue of Liberty. I want the New Liberal Indian to experience 'liberty' the way it should be.

The waves are swirling as I am very close to you now. Your face seems oddly familiar, though I have never encountered you before. We stand almost neck-to-neck now, eye-to-eye, staring. Your eyes are like a deer's, your lips curve so beautifully in your fair face. Your body is carved like mine, yet so much shapelier.

My eyes narrow as I see the same spot on your cheek as I have on mine. How do you look like that while I look like you? No, I am a mockery of you. Once again, the intensity of my desire to fuse with you overpowers.

This is the 'liberal' India of my dreams: eye-to-eye, confident, ready to face the world. This is the 'liberal' Indian of my dreams: similar to the 'liberal' India, with the same confidence and identical freedom. *Suddenly, it hits me. You smile your excruciating smile and I take one step ahead in awe. The waves wash over my head, finally enveloping my senses as we become one. I am you, and you are what I could have been. I breathe my last and I smile in peace fused with you, as now I walk in grace too!*

I am finally dead and like a phoenix from the ashes, I rise, fused with you, I am finally 'liberated' too.

10

JASH DHOLANI

Crumbling Empires of Dogma

Liberalism arose as an intellectual revolt against the oppressive stagnation of dogma. A time existed when entire swathes of people lived under warlords, when people fought and bled and faded away in search for tomorrow's breakfast, when to believe in a radical idea was to invite shame and death and oblivion. Darkness is not a natural master, and must invent threats to chain people's minds. Light, on the other hand, is the mistress of truth, and leads minds effortlessly into the world of freedom.

Freedom hasn't been the default condition of man for much of our history. The overbearing power of nature and the corrupt whims of tyrants restricted man's reach for millennia. There were places you couldn't go, people you couldn't mix with, things you couldn't think. It was too dangerous to venture out—the seas would swallow you if you sailed into the unknown, and the tyrants would execute you if you entertained a new notion. Religion, society, authority, death—these ravenous monsters roamed free as man's soul was chained and imprisoned and he was told to stay inside his dark little cell if he wanted to stay safe.

Safety, then, came at the cost of freedom, and man was a vulnerable little creature who crawled in the dim dusk of subsistence and flailed his limps helplessly, hoping to push his existence into a sicker tomorrow. In such a world, liberty was equivalent to danger, and danger was too costly a risk—it made sense to bow before the towering authority of the monarch, to stick religiously to the word of the prophet, to submit one's capacity to think before the imposing constructs of authority and steal in return a few more breaths, a little extra time. Life is addictive.

The dark, oppressive, highly illiberal days of the past were the way they were because of one reason: man's weakness. Floating in ignorance amidst vast seas of uncertainty, liberty was a luxury no man had a desire for. That changed, ever so slowly, in the 15th and 16th century as scientific progress metamorphosed into the industrial revolution, and unprecedented material progress empowered the individual to rebel against the empire of darkness and dogma. The power of the church and state, unshaken for centuries, was suddenly under threat—man no longer consented to living in swarms as an invisible cog in the machine, but wished his own motion, sought his own reason, and demanded his own liberty. Revolutions washed over the world.

Sun Rises in the West

Ten thousand years ago, a wall of fire had run over the forests of the world. Ancient man was burning trees by the millions to clear space for agriculture. We had been nomadic hunter-gatherers for much of our history. Nature had been chasing man threadbare for thousands of years, running his resources dry, and man had been forever on the run. But the discovery of growing our own food was going to change that. Man had stuck his feet in the ground, and planted a seed around his footprints. He was going to settle.

And settle he did. Communities flourished—groups of people started living together and the first rudimentary cities took shape. Humans had been around for many thousands of years, but the idea of humankind was slowly starting to form. Civilisation was about to emerge in all its infantile glory from the chaotic darkness of the past. And once it emerged, its growth was astronomical—we were the first species in the history of the planet to establish a society so complex in form and so varied in function. But there was a catch—emergence of the society led to a slow but unmistakable fall of the individual. Groups became more than the individuals they were composed of. Stagnation became the law of life. Pagan traditions had existed since long, but religion surfaced with all its ugly power and started dictating the terms of life. The nomad from the hunter-gatherer ages was a liberal, master of his own whims—but civilisation took his freedoms away. The tyranny of nature was replaced by a vaster tyranny of society. Groupthink became a norm, going with the herd a survival instinct. As the great German philosopher, Nietzsche, was to proclaim many millennia after, "Man had been degraded in the pursuit of mankind".

However, Nietzsche could be forgiven his pessimism because the industrial revolution which changed everything coincided with his lifetime and he didn't live to see its liberating effects. The 18th and the 19th century saw the creation of enormous wealth in the Western world as colonial powers took over the world and industrial production started and flourished at a previously unimaginable scale. Even as the Eastern societies slipped from the hands of native rulers and passed into the control of European masters, the Western man soared above the dirt ground of subsistence and knocked on the doors of luxury. Steam engine revolutionised transport, and the world wasn't so big anymore. Medical advances doubled the life expectancy, and man wasn't powerless before diseases anymore. Barter system collapsed as financial institutions took roots over much of Europe and America—money was invented and became an abstraction of all of man's desires. The individual, far oppressed in the yoke of collectivism, broke free from dogma and uncertainty, and sought refuge in knowledge and freedom. Renaissance washed over Europe as the church's monopoly on truth was shattered and free thought became every thinking man's right. America won its war of Independence, becoming the first capitalist state in the world—now selfishness was no longer a taboo and individual welfare and liberty were ideals worth chasing. It was not all smooth—blood was spilled and martyrs raised to the cause of liberty. But the cause survived. Light broke free. The sun of liberty had risen in the West.

The Eastern Elephant

India is one of the oldest civilisations in the world. The Indus Valley society rose and flourished on the banks of the river Indus, and was a pioneer among societies of the ancient world. Sanitation, wide roads, cultural recreations and a developed language—it had all the elements which a modern society of 2,000 years ago could boast of. The civilisation collapsed due to some unknown reason—historians are still divided over whether it was a flood, an external attack or some other unknown reason. Empires rose over the ashes of the Indus valley civilisation—empires sometimes as massive as the stretch over the breadth of the subcontinent. However, infighting between empires was frequent and a sense of national identity was nonexistent—India, for much of its history, was a collection of kingdoms looking to conquer increasing amounts of geographical area and not an integrated national unit existing as a unified whole. India was also one of the most economically vibrant places in the world and had quarter of the share of world trade—a fact that has more to do with India being one of the most populous countries in the world since always and less to do with any assumed specialty of the subcontinent. China, a neighbour to the north, used to enjoy economic significance similar to, and in some centuries more than India. This fact can again be attributed to sheer numbers—progress in the pre-industrial era was largely a result of having the maximum workers in agriculture and the cottage industries and less due to a differentiator like technology which became a factor later on.

India, for all its ancient roots and cultural wealth, has never been a society to value liberty. The concept of classical liberalism as it rose in the West was a negative concept—it was a negation of religion, negation of society, negation of external diktats. Individual, it was thought, had been chained by dogma, authority and tradition, and one had to negate all this—subtract all this—to return the autonomy to the individual. India, on the other hand, has always been a society in which the individual has been the dumping ground for the whims and fancies of the crowd. An individual is born in his caste, he has to defer before his tradition and all the endless rituals, he has to stay within his cultural limits, and he has to subdue his individual passions. He has to bow before his teachers, his parents, his gods—all authority figures built to stifle his freedom. He has responsibilities towards his family, his society, his environment—entities vague at best and undefined at worst. The whole thing has a spiritual code to it, but that doesn't make it less illiberal.

A Half Tilted Domino

World's largest democracy. Second largest economy. Most populous nation on earth. Biggest population of young people. Biggest population of poor people. India is not one nation, but nations upon nations—it's not one society or culture, but many of them interwoven in complex formations.

The idea of liberty, then, or rather the betrayal of it, manifests itself in different forms. Officially India claims to be the world's largest democracy, and still we have rationalists being murdered and artists chased out of the country for the crime of speaking their minds. The politicians stand for no liberal principles but rather succumb to the fads of their electorate. The government disregards civil liberties with astonishing frequency—the recent meat ban being an example. The food habits of the people of the world's largest democracy are subject, apparently, to the shifting moralities of the politicians. People are worried that it's a recent trend, but the reality is scarier—it's not. From the imposition of Emergency in the 1970s to the mysterious murders of opposition leaders at both state and national levels, from the banning of Salman Rushdie's *Satanic Verses* to M.F. Husain getting death threats over his paintings, the Indian state has a spectacular track record of neither respecting nor maintaining the liberties of Indians. Rushdie was denied an Indian visa for 12 years, and M.F. Husain died away from home. We, as a political nation-state, have given lip service to the ideals of democracy while letting our liberals, our artists, and our countrymen down.

As we shift our gaze from politics to society and culture, it assumes an added air of futility. At the political level, there is at least a pretence of being democratic. We might be rated 28th on the Democracy Index and tagged a "flawed democracy", but that phrase has the word 'democracy' in it. Gunmen might be gunning down rationalists in open daylight, but we do not accept extra judicial killings as morally right. On the other hand, outside the political sphere, in the realms of society and culture, we've accepted highly dogmatic beliefs as principles to live by and don't make adequate if any efforts to challenge them. Discrimination against women, parents choosing the careers and life partners of their children, caste boundaries in housing and workplaces—these are all realities we've observed and grown numb to. They doesn't strike us as illiberal—they strike us as natural. The way things have always been. And worse—the way things should always be. Instead of facing the regressive reality of our society, we bask in our imagined glory. The state of research in Indian universities is pathetic, but it is okay because Aryabhatta invented Zero 1500 years back. The crimes against women are taking an increasingly appalling shape, but it is okay because we worship female goddesses. Our society actively suppresses individual liberty, but it is okay because social harmony comes first and we must protect the sanctity of a rotten culture that celebrates collectivism.

The area where lack of liberty hurts the most, though, and where its brazen ill effects are most severely felt, is the economy. There are four factors of production—land, labour, capital and entrepreneurship—and all four are deeply entrenched in the shackles of the Indian regulatory state. Acquiring land, a primary requirement for creation of a manufacturing economy, is a nightmare in India. Moreover, property rights were devolved from a fundamental right to a mere legal right in 1978, and after that the citizens of India no longer have had the right to file a Supreme Court writ in case of an infringement of their property rights. Labour laws are a mess, and make it impossible for employers to hire and fire and for workers to have the mobility needed to be prosperous in a developing country. Complex contracts, unrealistic compensation requirements, and a deeply complacent and corrupt bureaucracy make it impossible for free market forces to appropriately allocate land and labour. Capital remains expensive in India, and there are caps on how much foreign investment is allowed in different sectors. Entrepreneurship remains a risk against the odds in a hostile environment. Tariffs, protectionism and restraints on free trade make India rank a dismal 128th on the economic freedom index—below Kenya, Botswana and Ghana.

What does it mean to be a liberal in India, then? To be a liberal in India means to be the frustrated voice in a lonely opinion piece. To be a little letter to the editor, peripheries marked by stains of tea cups. To be a liberal in India means to speak a language alien to your surroundings. Liberalism has been, in retrospect, divided into classical liberalism and social liberalism, and India fails miserably on both accounts. Classical liberalism propagates freedom of speech, negation of the big government and free market economies, and India is miles and decades away from fitting the bare minimums of that definition. Social liberalism believes in adequate education and healthcare, freedom from disease and poverty, and swift social justice—and India, being a third world country, even with its massive welfare mechanisms, has had damning failures in its efforts to provide citizens with the above. Both classical and social liberals can and do join ranks to rant about India and its devastating betrayals of the liberal ideals. This is not the tryst with destiny we dreamt of.

This, then, is the reality of the day—India is a half tilted domino. Liberty as an essential political doctrine has washed over and been accepted in major parts of the world, but it has had a tough time penetrating the cultural xenophobia and economic protectionism of our homeland. We aspire to a future with our feet deeply entrenched in the limitations of the past. We take pledges to liberty and revel in the music of our rattling cages. A young generation has come up—ambitious, restless and lost. Will we use our demographic dividend before it turns a liability? Will we reform our democracy before it slips into regression and becomes a mere shadow of our collective dream? Which way will the domino tilt? The decades lying in front of us, the decades of tantalising uncertainty and golden hope, hold the answer.

11

N.R. PRASHANTH BHAT

Taking Responsibility: Being a Liberal in India

> Where liberty dwells, there is my country.
>
> —Milton

On 26th November 1949, the Constituent Assembly of India adopted the Preamble of the Constitution which reads as follows:

> WE THE PEOPLE OF INDIA, having solemnly resolved to constitute India into a SOVERIGN DEMOCRATIC REPUBLIC and to secure all its citizens: JUSTICE: social, economic and political; LIBERTY: of thought expression, belief and faith; EQUALITY: of status and of opportunity and to promote among them all FRATERNITY assuring the dignity of the individual and the unity and integrity of the nation.

The framers of the Indian Constitution, many of who were influenced by western intellectual and political thought, have incorporated several liberal principles in the charter. These include freedom of speech, life, expression, association, movement and of residence, right to practice and promote religion peacefully, right against exploitation and the rule of law. Though the Indian Constitution borrowed heavily from Western conventions, there was no blind adoption of their ideals. Many of the provisions were modified to suit the Indian context. The framers envisaged a bright and prosperous future for the country under these liberal values. Though the directive principles of state policy enshrined in the Constitution had a socialist slant, they were clearly reluctant to include socialism in the Preamble while charting the future of India post-independence. It was only in 1976, that the words “Socialist” and “Secular” were inserted into the Preamble by the government led by Indira Gandhi through the 42nd amendment.

The Importance of Being a Liberal in India

As evidenced by the Preamble, the framers of the Constitution took cognizance of the challenges Indian society faced at that time which included untouchability, communalism, caste-based discrimination, and ethnic, linguistic and cultural diversity. They saw subscription to liberal values as the only way India could survive as a pluralist nation. The core libertarian principles of refraining from harming the rights of other people, respecting the rules of justice and standing up for the rights of others were considered essential for peaceful social-cooperation in a country where caste, religious, regional and linguistic fault lines were deep rooted.

Circa 2015, India's social challenges continue to persist. National and regional political parties which see an opportunity in the existing fault lines, amplify them to stoke fear among communities and harness votes. Consequently, India continues to suffer communal strife, caste-related violence, linguistic fights and conflicts between states which as the conventional wisdom suggests, deters investment and economic growth. Social violence destroys lives and livelihoods, spreads mutual hatred and insecurity among people, affects production and distribution of goods and stalls economic activity.

In fact, economic growth and social violence have a very symbiotic mutualistic relationship. A recent study by scholars at the University of British Columbia concluded that for every 1 per cent increase in the GDP growth rate, the expected number of riots and social violence decreases by 5 per cent.[1]

While economic growth acts as an antidote to social violence, the growth itself is predicated upon social harmony and peace. Also, in the case of India, the stakes are very high. Half of India's children below the age of five are malnourished and a bulk of Indians (over 29.5%) remain desperately poor.[2] Over 25 per cent of the Indians are still illiterate and the unemployment rate is constantly on the rise. It is true that millions of people have been lifted from poverty in the

1. Bohlken, Anjali Thomas (2010). "Economic Growth and Ethnic Violence: An Empirical Investigation of Hindu-Muslim Riots in India", *Journal of Peace Research*, 28 September.

2. Government of India, Ministry of Home Affairs, *Census 2011*.

last two decades, thanks to economic liberalisation. But for these reforms to succeed and yield desired results, a peaceful and conducive atmosphere is a necessary pre-condition which can only be achieved by mutual respect, tolerance and upholding the rule of law.

With 430 million people in the country within the age of 15 and 34 looking for jobs and opportunities, the consequences of underdevelopment will prove to be disastrous. Hence, it is all the more important for Indians to adhere to liberal values of tolerance, peace and dignity of each individual without which it is impossible to grow economically. The state can contribute in fostering this social harmony by enforcing the rules of just conduct, protecting well-defined individual rights and applying law equally to all the people.

Social Liberal *versus* Classical Liberal

Who is an Indian liberal? This is an important question to address because there are many policy makers, media personalities, academicians and public-intellectuals who are self-declared inheritors of liberal tradition. Interestingly, their idea of liberalism is very different from its classical sense. While classical liberalism supports freedom for an individual in all aspects—political, personal and economic, social liberals confine themselves to advocating only personal and political freedoms.

The concept of social liberalism emerged in the late-19th century with T.H. Green's distinction between positive and negative liberty. Giving themselves various nomenclatures such as "left-liberal" or "modern-liberal", they brush aside economic freedom and even despise capitalism and the free-market economy. They have a tendency to seek state intervention in providing social and economic services and sometimes even support extreme socialism.

For instance, in India, they rightfully oppose government's ban on books, movies and literature which curtail free speech and individual right to access them. But they also oppose land and labour reforms and deregulation of the economy, condemning such moves as being 'anti-poor' even though there is enough evidence to the contrary. Economic, personal and political freedoms are inseparable. One without the other two or vice-versa cannot make a society truly free. In fact, most of the times, economic freedom can advance political and personal liberties.

For example, millions of Indians consumed the content produced by India's public broadcaster Doordarshan for over three decades after televisions were first introduced in India. It fed viewers information that was mostly filled with government propaganda. People watched news that government wanted them to because they had no other choice. There was very little if any space left for the opposition's views in the content produced by the state broadcaster. It was only after the advent of private news channels that the opposition parties in India got their fair share of television news space and a platform to freely express their views and opinions. So, the arrival of competitive markets broke the state monopoly and led to free flow of ideas and created space for dissenting voices which were hitherto neglected and overlooked.

In yet another example of how economic freedom facilitates personal liberty, a survey study conducted in two districts of Uttar Pradesh state found major changes in the lifestyles of Dalits (once called the untouchables considered the lowest in the caste-hierarchy) since the opening up of the Indian economy in 1990. In Azhamgarh district, the proportion of Dalits not seated separately at non-Dalit weddings has gone up from 22.7 per cent in 1990 to 68.4 per cent in 2007. In the same district, the number of Dalits living in brick houses has gone up from 18.1 per cent in 1990 to 46.3 per cent in 2007.[3] Market reforms and subsequent creation of wealth and opportunities has enabled Dalits to get out of their historical occupations like cleaning toilets and cremating the dead, and move into new occupations.

In defining Indian liberals, it is extremely important to make this distinction between modern/social and classical liberals. One is either a liberal in political civil and economic spheres or not. Selective liberalism with absolute disregard and even contempt to economic

---

3. Kapur, Devesh Chandra Bhan Prasad, Lant Pritchett and D ShyamBabu (2010). "Rethinking Inequality: Dalits in Uttar Pradesh in the Market Reform Era", in *Economic & Political Weekly* XLV(35), 28 August.

freedom is an attempt to obfuscate pseudo-liberalism with the classical one.

For over four decades after India attained its political freedom in 1947, Indians were restrained by the clutches of the state which created a Soviet-style 'command economy' or what is now popularly known as 'license raj'. Permits were required for all economic activity. As a result, investments by private businesses declined significantly. Fabian socialist policies and 'mixed' economy models have led to low foreign investments and missed opportunities thereby denying India the benefits of international technology and foreign competition. High-level corruption, malfeasance and inefficiency had become common in unreformed sectors which were dominated by government enterprises.

With absolute monopoly and state control, no accountability or competition, the government got away with providing shoddy public services in telecommunications, transport, power and infrastructure sectors. Unemployment and poverty were natural byproducts of such a system. As a result, the quality of life in India remained poor.

Conversely, lifestyles of most Indians improved drastically after the market liberalisation in 1990. In 1994, the country witnessed a GDP growth rate of 5.9 per cent which reached 8.6 per cent by 2005-2007.[4] The openness in the economy enhanced the rate of investment at home, which in turn led to high economic growth. The number of people below the poverty line was reduced from 403.7 million in 1990 to 269.3 million in 2011 despite the growth in overall population of the country during the same time period.[5]

Such an impressive growth was possible only because of India's integration with the world economy and adoption of market-oriented development policies. By choosing individual empowerment as a transformative strategy for poverty eradication, the country made significant socio-economic progress in a short span of time. This reaffirms F.A. Hayek's assessment that centralisation of economic

---

4. Panagariya, Arvind (2008). *India: The Emerging Giant*. Oxford University Press p.108
5. Planning Commission (2013). *Press note on Poverty Estimates, 2011-12*. Government of India. July.

powers with the government could undermine political and civil liberties.

Therefore, it is even more important to distinguish between classical liberals and social liberals before the latter destroy the very ideals liberalism originated to promote.

Being a Liberal in India: Taking Responsibility

> Stand up, be bold, be strong. Take the whole responsibility on your own shoulders, and know that you are the creator of your own destiny. All the strength and succor you want is within yourself. Therefore make your own future.
>
> —Swami Vivekananda

The process of economic reform in India is incomplete or is work-in-progress as some might want to see it. Although the license and quota raj have for most part come to an end, the inspector raj continues. Government officials often use their discretionary powers to harass small entrepreneurs, street vendors, industrialists and factory owners for bribes. The prospect of public officials starting from sales tax officers to police inspectors knocking on their doors for bribes, dissuades many people from becoming entrepreneurs. Corruption is ubiquitous in sectors which are still under government control. This has been corroborated by the recent multi-million dollar coal-mining scam where large scale corruption has been reported in the allocation of coal blocks.

The rule of law is poorly enforced in the country. With more than 30 million cases pending trial in the Indian courts, pursuit of justice can be an incredibly painful process. Our public healthcare system is in disarray and our law enforcement methods have not been modernised in years.

Since the solution to most of these problems lies with the government, it is important for us to elect better politicians to public office. As Eleanor Roosevelt had once said, “with freedom comes responsibility,” for liberals to enjoy freedom, it is important to fulfil their responsibility by exercising their rights as citizens, to vote during elections. The urban middle-class population in India which is much more aware about policy related issues, doesn’t vote as much as it should. For instance, only 58.81 per cent of voters in Bengaluru city voted during the 2014-Loksabha elections. If citizens remain passive and don't vote, they lose their moral right to complain about endemic corruption and governance issues.

Secondly, young and educated liberals must contribute their time and energy to enlighten people about the implications of public policies. Educating people through social media platforms, blogs or news articles about the nexus between hardened criminals and corrupt politicians, will help shape public opinion and enable them to make informed choices during elections.

Good governance is possible only through active citizen participation. Liberals must volunteer at the grass-roots levels to take charge of their own lives. Planting trees, cleaning-up the streets, spreading awareness on hygiene and sanitation in their neighbourhood and coming up with innovative ideas to decrease the community's reliance on government can go a long way in lifting living standards and minimising corruption.

Lastly, being a liberal means to take the ultimate responsibility and risk of joining politics. The educated middle-class doesn't have a good opinion on politicians. That is precisely why a liberal must join politics. After all, more preaching will not change the mindset of people and politicians. If a liberal can capsule a powerful message to the aspirational middle-class voters and get elected to the public office it is possible to bring political and administrative reforms to substantially eradicate corruption.

Competition, choice and technology which were outcomes of liberalisation closed many avenues of corruption in India. But several new avenues for corruption opened up in the recent past because the reforms that started in 1991 remain incomplete and the state is reluctant to modernise its public services. This is all the more reason why Indian liberals must take on the mantle of fighting corruption through active political participation. After all, Swami Vivekananda had rightly said more than 100 years ago, "we are the creators of our own destiny."'

12

SREYOSHI GUHA

Struggles of a Closet Idealist

In the India of today, it is not surprising to wake up to the news of our Hon'ble Prime Minister sharing a warm bear hug with the President of the UAE—discussing prospects for further development of positive bilateral relations. And then, somewhere not far below in the same newspaper, blending with the black and white of the familiar text is news of another woman raped somewhere in the shrubberies of her neighbourhood; another inter-caste couple hanged from a tree; another teen taking his own life—unable to face family 'pressure' or unable to step out of the closet or maybe even, simply put: unable to conform to the established norms of a confused society.

When asked, what being a liberal in India, means to me: I see through the eyes of a closet idealist. I see the problems of a society straining to embrace modernity and change, all the while unable to let go of a bygone era. The India of today is shadowed in a hypocrisy disguised as tradition and norm. Through the eyes of the average closet idealist, I see liberalism as a struggle between what I am and what I want to be.

> I may disagree with what you have to say, but I will defend to the death your right to say it.
>
> Voltaire[1]

To the average closet idealist, waking up every morning in this teeming democracy of 1.3 billion people brings a quiet sigh to go with the morning *chai*. The continual defence of all that is good and beautiful falls short with the coming of the morning newspaper.

1. As postulated by Hall, Evelyn Beatrice (1906). *The Friends of Voltaire*.

Sexual violence, crime in the name of religion, ban on food items—the list is endless.

The India of today struggles at a fundamental level. There is something it wishes to be and then something it really is. The bygone era with its unforgiving pride of culture and tradition refuses to let go of a nation, which, in spirit has long since leapt forward and beyond—onto that charming new world that modernity brings.

The result? A fizzing, gurgling, explosive mass of political confusion, social misdirection and just the stark contrast of reality with theory. This is the India of today, the India of the newspapers, the India that is marketed globally as the 'next best thing.'

As a student of political science and eventually of law, I would agree with the definition of liberalism that describes it as a doctrine that is concerned primarily with the protection and enhancement of individual liberty. Laski, a political philosopher says, "Liberalism is the expression less of a trend rather than of a temperament. It implies a passion for liberty. It requires a power to be tolerant; yet skeptical about opinions and tendencies you hold to be dangerous".

A moment's perusal of the above leads to the assumption that liberalism concerns itself with two things: a) liberty and b) the individual.

Which ever context you choose to study this ideal in, it is these two basic constituents that matter—their perceptions, definitions, effects and scope. What is liberty? What is individual liberty? It is important to add here that different interpretations and variations of the ideal would witness inclinations to either ends of the aforementioned spectrum. There are those that identify liberalism more with individualism, prioritising the individual and his/her rights over any and all state control. There are others, who emphasise the importance of state control in protecting and enhancing individual liberty. Whatever the different types and inclinations may be, at the centre of liberalism is the individual's liberty and every liberal not only understands that, but also respects, recognises and defends it in practice.

Being a liberal, therefore, is a lot more than just the commonplace perception of simply being open minded and accepting. With all its tenets and dynamics intact, liberalism and being liberal should be that zenith of celebration for individual liberty that creates a society of ultimate freedom—whatever it may mean to an individual.

The Indian Context

As a nation, as a people, we suffer from an inherent contradiction of being. Wherever you go: whether it is out on to the streets for a walk, sharing a loud evening around the living room with family members, or even if you were to buy something from the neighbourhood grocery store—there is a contradiction of theory and practice, of what is and what should be. Decades ago, when the Constituent Assembly sat itself down for months on end to draft the Constitution of the nation, it looked to the visibly 'modern' West and borrowed everything that would help it shake off the colonial past and become new, polished and different. It was said that everything that was borrowed was wisely fitted into the 'Indian context' to create a unique constitution—complete with the assets of tested democracies in a new-born, diverse democracy which had the bonus blessing of tradition and culture. The Constitution in theory, guaranteed "personal liberty" under Article 21 along with the right to life. It granted freedoms, albeit with reasonable restrictions, under Article 19. What it probably did not anticipate, was the confusion that this 'Indian context' would create. The problem is when freedom of speech broadly grants you the freedom to criticise your government but the same government would easily arrest you for it.[2] The problem when secular legislation clashes with personal laws. The problem when the solution to violence against women is that they dress traditionally.[3] The problem when the large masses of people conveniently forget that true freedom is freedom from all fears and being liberal is to

2. "Girls' FB Post Gets Them Arrested," *Hindustan Times*, *http://www.hindustantimes.com/mumbai/girls-fb-posts-get-them-arrested/article1-961478.aspx*. Accessed on 15 September 2015.

3. "Akhil Bharat Hindu Mahasabha Warns Girls: 'Vulgar Clothes Lead to Rape; Wants Ban on Jeans, Cell Phones", *The Financial Express*, *http://www.financialexpress.com/article/miscellaneous/akhil-bharat-hindu-mahasabha-warns-irls-vulgar-clothes-lead-to-rape-wants-ban-on-jeans-cell-phones/14246/*. Accessed on 15 September 2015.

advocate that world where every individual lives with that ultimate freedom from fear.

In the 21st century, the world understands freedom in various manifestations. Globalisation has encouraged a further integration of national concepts with international ones. Whether one likes it or not, the economy continues to demand better allegiance to interconnectedness—both politically and socially. This, of course, has been furthered by social media. The Indian youth therefore, has ideas and notions different from those of the generations preceding them. The Indian youth wants to be liberal, like their international counterparts. He/she is constantly shaped by the ideas that he/she can relate to, that often are not the ones encouraged at home. It is these various manifestations of freedom that can be used to highlight what being a liberal means in the Indian context.

Homosexuality: The Eternal Example

Earlier this year, when the US Supreme Court legalised same-sex marriages,[4] there was celebration all around. Love, it seems, had won. In India, too, the judgement was celebrated with rainbow coloured display pictures on Facebook[5] and status updates etched with triumph. Everyone seemed, for a moment, to forget that here in India, coming out of the closet will still attract negative judgement. The stigma attached to being queer is not only real but takes away your basic freedom of sexual orientation. A country that criminalises a sexual act between two consenting male adults[6] is, to me, far from recognising true personal liberty.

In this context, being a liberal would take you to the court in argument for the rights of homosexuals just to be blatantly told that you live in a country where sex between two males is unnatural and therefore, criminal. Here, being a liberal would lead you into constant debates with friends and peers just to realise that there is no real

4. Obergefell v. Hodges, 135 S. Ct. 2584.

5. Solomon, Diana Beth (2015). "World Web Brightens with Rainbows Celebrating Same Sex Marriages", *Los Angeles Times*, *http://www.latimes.com/business/la-fi-tn-social-media-rainbows-20150626-story.html*. Accessed on 15 September 2015.

6. Section 377, Indian Penal Code, 1860.

point: you cannot change a stubbornness validated by society. In India, being a liberal would be to find in the course of these numerous arguments—self-proclaimed 'liberals' who proudly announce how they have no 'problem' with homsexuals but just don't want to have anything to do with it. They do not realise that their complacency or averse attitude towards it culminates in a society that sneers and scoffs and potentially puts homosexuals behind bars for nothing more than being who they are.

Feminism: The Misunderstood Agenda

In concept and definition, feminism simply means the equality of sexes. Which ever sphere of life you choose, you should be equal to the opposite sex. Feminism was a movement that was begun to uplift the position of women in society. It was necessary, not just in India, but around the world to battle the ill-effects of a well-established patriarchy. True equality can only be achieved if both parties are placed on a level playing field. And any 13 year old will be able to tell you, that often privileges and benefits are required to create this level playing field. Positive discrimination, if you will which is, once again, guaranteed by the Indian Constitution.

One could argue, as I often have before I truly understood it, that feminism is an outdated movement. Women are heading MNCs, they are no longer confined to domestic spheres. Women are competing equally with men for jobs. Women have rights equal to those of their male counterparts—she is no longer oppressed, she is no longer the 'weaker' sex, she is empowered and emancipated. One could argue that feminism favours women in a social context that has already achieved equality between men and women; that feminism makes man the villain.

A liberal would understand that when a woman is raped, patriarchy wins. He/she would perceive that every time a woman walks out on the street and is eve teased or molested, she is placed back into that social spectrum that considers her status subsidiary to the man's. A liberal would see that despite being protected in theory and law, the woman is subject to a patriarchal mindset that takes away her freedom from fear. This mindset needs feminism. A mindset that treats both the sexes equally would not only refrain from disrespecting a woman, but would stand up to those that do.

Being a liberal in India is to be in support of women's rights and yet, turn a blind eye to sexual harassment right before your eyes. It is to accept it in theory, but succumb to patriarchy every day, in practice. It is to roll your eyes at the minister on TV, who verbally disrespects women in an official statement but forget that it is we who elected him, our mindset that granted him the confidence and power to say it and get away with it.

Secularism

India practices a secularism different from the West. The US would define secularism as a complete separation of church and state.[7] In India, however, secularism is to "practice, profess and propagate" any religion of your choice—with equal freedom.[8] Religion, in this case, finds positive expression in the State.[9]

The result of this secularism is a plethora of personal laws that are unto themselves wholly untouched spheres. It is a well-established concept that any law, if in conflict with a personal law will be defeated as far as it contradicts it. The direct effect of this is the defeat of a number of well-meaning, forward looking laws.

The liberal in India would grasp the true meaning of this discrepancy and drop his head in submission. The liberal in India would not be able to explain to this 'tradition' obsessed nation that religion is best confined to the personal space—that when it moves beyond that, it becomes vicious and unforgiving, taking away the individual freedoms of many. The liberal in India would struggle with secularism as a concept. "Protect, profess and propagate," such liberal would say, does not mean at the lengths of infringing someone else's freedom. Freedom to follow it differently, freedom to choose a different religion, and even the freedom to not follow any religion

---

7. Kuru, Ahmet T. (2009). "Secularism and State Policies toward Religion: The United States, France & Turkey", *Cambridge Studies in Social Theory, Religion and Politics*, April.
8. Art 25-26, Constitution of India, 1950.
9. 42nd amendment to the preamble includes the word "secular". "Secularism" part of basic structure of the Constitution; S.R. Bommai v. Union of India [1994] 2 SCR 644.

at all. The liberal in India who tried to achieve the above would be branded an atheist, a misfortune, a liability.

Stereotypes: The Real Enemy of Liberalism

As a country, we have moved beyond caste and class in many ways. In theory and in practice—to a large extent. The shadow of stereotypes and its true effect, however, still looms low and dangerous over the nation that claims to have left them far behind. It could be anything: class, caste, gender, religion, ethnicity, and even opportunities. As a student, I see stereotypes in the limited career options presented to peers or friends or even family members, by their families. I hear random statements thrown carelessly across dinner tables about the misfortunes of belonging to a particular religion, different from one's own. "Stop crying! Stop behaving like a girl", I hear often.

The liberal in India succumbs to stereotypes every day. The Indian liberal discusses rights and with a head held high sneers at conservatism in form and type; and yet would not allow his domestic help to use the same spoon as his. The real enemy of progress is the culmination of a mindset that has closed all doors to change and liberalism. Stereotype is without basis and logic; it is unaccepting and often unforgiving. It is not always light and laughable, it is also deep and intrinsic—affecting the personal liberty of many. The liberal in India is yet to recognise this, to understand that true liberty can only be achieved where the mind is free.

Hypocrisy: The Indian Liberal's True Struggle

The Indian society, whether we like it or not, is hypocritical. The contradiction between theory and practice results in a hypocrisy that India itself is not entirely aware of. There are times we can look beyond it, joke about it and let it slip, unnoticed beneath the bed. Then there are times when it disguises itself into the main road block to progress and development. The liberal in India is one who combats this inherent hypocrisy every day and, to a large extent, fails. The liberal in India prides him/herself for being ahead of the conservative but does not see, in all the bloated pride, who really gets the last laugh.

To the average closet idealist, all of the above would be synonymous to the odd bitterness of morning *chai* that has been boiled for a tad bit too long. And then somewhere in the teeming democracy of 1.3 billion people a transgender becomes the principal of a school,[10] Jains speak up against meat ban,[11] men stand up for feminism, religious differences are locked outside the cricket stadium. To the average closet idealist, a slow peace of mind returns. With time, she too will learn to perfect her morning *chai*.

---

10. Premanukar Biswas, "West Bengal College Welcomes India's First Transgender Principal", *The Indian Express, http://indianexpress.com/article/india/west-bengal-college-welcomes-indias-first-transgender-principal/*. Accessed on 15 September, 2015.

11. Krishandas Rajkumar, "Mumbai Meat Ban Raises Key Constitutional Questions", *The Hindu, http://www.thehindu.com/news/national/mumbai-meat-ban-raises-key-constitutional-question/article7646589.ece*. Accessed on 15 September, 2015.

13

TANMAYI GIDH

Being Liberal: Embracing the Change

I find myself at an oddly amusing and amusingly difficult juncture in life. As I write this, I am already imagining the reactions of the number of people who would read this. And maybe even the criticism. I think I'm more intimidated by the latter. Although I keep reminding myself, my job is to put forth what I feel, honestly. The rest isn't up to me.

Can I, though? Can we put forth a view without the apprehension of how it would be received? Would it conform, would it please, would it be understood? It is a tough job separating your views from those of the society. And that is what I have been having a tough time dealing with these days.

Being a student of a highly interactive and proactive philosophy department, I often carry a lot of uncomfortable questions home for company. Out of the many words like Epicureanism, Ontology, Liberation, Liberalism flying about the department, a lot of which I miss, some words, some ideas, some questions stick. When you begin to question what has been largely accepted, clear your mind of everything that has accumulated over the years as beliefs, truths, ideas, something within you and how you see the world changes. Slowly those classroom discussions grow on you and you begin to consciously question the established meanings of a lot of societal concepts, and their unfortunate exploitation. And liberalism is one of those.

Now before I began expressing what being a liberal means to me, I looked up the universally accepted definition of being a liberal. Because that is one of the places where we go wrong. We tend to bend the ideas a little to fit ourselves in its context. And then some more. Still a little more maybe... until it is our idea of the original one.

So, one of the definitions of being liberal is: i) Favouring reform, not bound by traditional thinking. Willing to respect or accept behaviour or opinions different from one's own; open to new ideas.

Hold on. Where did my right to my freedom of thought, religion, my ideas of a perfect society, my non-conformism go? Why does it find no room in the definition? That was precisely where I went wrong earlier on. For me, being a liberal was being convictional and open about my ideas, (of course they had to essentially be opposed to the conventionally held views, or what's the point?); furthermore, it was trying to convince everyone that that was the 'only' right view to hold.

Another definition of liberal is: ii) Propounding social or political liberalism.

A governing structure where the number of freedoms—that of expression, thought, religion, etc., become an essential part of the society, given equally to all.

In a country like India, largely driven by a right-wing regime, in present day conditions more than ever, we need to bring about a change, not merely at a schematic level but at an ideological level. Where our religious, social and cultural diversity is not merely an aspect but a matter of pride, ensuring conditions suitable for this diversity to flourish are unquestionable. A balance needs to be sought to establish both, equity and equality.

And finally, whom would you call a liberal?

A person of liberal views.

In a society that holds interpersonal relations, religious and communistic adherence and interdependence in such high regard, it is difficult to separate an individual identity. It is further difficult to respect that individual identity without crossing the thin line to being individualistic.

I have been brought up in an environment more different, more liberal than what most Indian kids grow up in. I was never kept from picking any piece of literature I wanted, and it opened my mind to radically contrasting views from those I held and invariably also influenced and shaped my ideas. The urge to open my heart to lives and minds different from mine was strengthened as I grew up and continued to travel across geographies—coasts to mountains to forests; cultures—from my extended family and across continents; ideologies—aristocratic to democratic, and themes—sceptic to teleological.

Do I find myself incredibly fortunate for being able to look at the world with these eyes?—Incredibly! Would I propound the attitude?—Not unless you have a strong stomach.

Because as I grew up, I realised I had bargained for more than free thought and free will, which was now inherently ingrained in me. Being a liberal was a conscious choice of standing up for my beliefs and values. It was also a choice to reason with contradictory views and stomach the condemnation and condescendence that came with the failure of being able to do so. It was committing to a lifetime of doubt and insecurity. It was about having the courage to swallow the very words I fought for on being proven wrong. Being a liberal is just as much about standing down as it is about standing for. It is about raising uncomfortable questions, refusing to conform to the crowd mentality, living life on your own terms. There is the feeling of being associated with the thinking class, yet also the isolation of belonging to no one—neither your religion nor relations. Because our approach towards our ideas guides every aspect of our lives, and I wouldn't accept anything on its face value.

Being liberal is also, essentially about 'acceptance' of views other than (if not opposite) yours—being able to view different ideas objectively, yet with a conscious consideration, with sympathy, with empathy. Always keeping in mind that nothing, no person, no value, no knowledge is merely a means but an end in itself. And in return, you can only hope that maybe you could move the society to at least accept these differences, if not embrace them. There are always people who are less fortunate compared to us, but there are also those far better off. Whatever the case, we are responsible not only for our condition but for that of the remaining classes as well.

We are a nation of a billion. We're not only billion individuals but also a billion ideas. We're a billion ideas suppressed under the demands of employment, community and politics. Our government is struggling to assure the invariable equality that our Constitution guarantees. The ridge between the extremes in any socio-political aspect is a significant hurdle. However, our willingness to act for the benefit of those living in conditions different from ours is an equal cause. In a democracy, where we choose whom we're run by, our government is a reflection of us. The stagnancy in terms of reforms, the socio-political instability owing the clash among classes, the economic ridge between the rich and the poor, the religious intolerance and a hundred other issues that grapple us at a national level are severely etched within us at an individual and societal level as well.

We, as a country and as individuals, are at a juncture where we need to look beyond our immediate concerns and our immediate comforts. It is time to bury the hatchets and take people for being people! As was mentioned in *To Kill a Mockingbird,* "There's only one kind of folks, folks!" Then what makes us build these walls between us? It takes courage to move beyond the animosity and indifference that has been unconsciously embedded into us over the years; but in doing do, we're opening our hearts and minds to a whole new world of change and progress—as humans and as a society.

The cities won't clean themselves. The class distinctions wouldn't be overcome by themselves. Corruption won't fight itself. The equality won't be established by itself. The ridge won't destroy itself. The guilty won't punish themselves. We won't wake up one fine day to a superpower, our Utopian idea of a state. We all need change, desperately—at an ideological level, at a societal level. Only thing is, we wouldn't work for it until our graver worries don't come and stare us in our faces, until they don't begin to pinch us directly. Being a liberal is looking this change in its face, and being willing to embrace it, expanding our horizons for the greater good.

More than being a supporter of reformations and liberalism, we are required to be its propagator. Being a liberal, for me, isn't a school of thought or a state of mind, it is a journey—with a long and winding road to walk upon, and a beautiful view at each bend.

14

UTKARSH SRIVASTAVA

The Indian Liberal: A Subjective Approach

It is impossible to write an essay which covers all Indian liberals. Quite simply because liberalism means too many things to too many people. There is no one-size-fits-all definition which would work for everyone. And there really shouldn't be. Because liberalism is a system of beliefs. And humans, being humans, must each have their own convictions and beliefs. In the present context, these ideas are those regarding as to how, if at all, we should be governed. We all have different ideas of how that should happen. As we very well should. It is after all what makes us an 'intelligent' specie.

And yet, there aren't enough thoughts in the world for each of us to have entirely unique belief systems. In broad strokes, we agree with a large number of people around the world as to what our system of governance should be.

Liberalism is one way to do it. In very general terms, it is the idea of individual freedom. It is the idea of self-governance. It is the idea of letting grown-ups be grown-ups. While it is certainly hard to pigeonhole the idea of liberalism given the various strains and types of liberalism prevalent around the world, there is still a consensus on some general points which liberals would subscribe to. Liberalism supports the freedom of speech and information, secularism, civil rights, democracies and free markets. It is against discriminating (positively or negatively) on the basis of birth, and the interference by the State into the lives of the citizens.

Indians are a curious case study in liberalism. Even though the civilisation which forms our backbone is thousands of years old, the nation as it is today, is a relatively young one. Only after the British yoke was lifted from our shoulders and we undertook our 'tryst with destiny', could we really start taking decisions which would define us as a nation.

As it happened, the men and women taking decisions at those nascent stages of our democracy were by and large liberals. The Indian National Congress was the collective which was at the fore in the struggle for independence. And the Congress was, and remains, a liberal party by any measure. And what else could it be? For independence struggles are by and large the domain of liberals as their pursuit of individual freedoms often requires them to fight for the collective freedom of their country as well.

The Constitutional Assembly, again a collective in which liberals had the majority, gave us the Fundamental Rights. These are the embodiment of our civil rights. Even though they are but a few in number, they form the fountainhead of Indian human rights as rights ranging from environment to privacy have been read into them.

With such a vast history of liberalism there is a legitimate expectation from India to carry on the liberal tradition. And yet, the party currently in power is a collective of right-wing conservatives. That party, the Bharatiya Janata Party (BJP) has had previous trysts with power too. It is in this context that we must understand the Indian liberal.

Power to the People?

India is not a democracy in the truest sense of the world. To be fair, neither is the USA or the UK or any of the progressive European nations. This is because true democracy is a myth. To attain true democracy, we must take the Athenian model of direct democracy where all citizens were part of the legislative process and apply it without the exclusions that went with it. The Athenian model excluded large portions of the populace including women, slaves etc. A true democracy would extend the Athenian model to everyone in the country.

That idea of democracy remains unattainable for a number of reasons not the least of which are logistics and lack of interest. It would truly take something spectacular to usher in the era of democracy as it should be. Until that happens however, there will a centre of power called the State. The State will take certain decisions keeping in mind the good of the nation as a whole (the greater good, if you will). Now these decisions are always trade-offs. This is due to the large number of people these decisions affect. Many people would benefit from the decision and many will be worse off. The economist would argue that a good decision would then be one which benefits more people than it harms.

Except, it isn't always that easy. The idea that a benevolent State would take decisions which it knows very well will harm a section of the populace is itself a case study in ethical dilemmas. These could be people that elected the people who govern in the first place. And the number of these people could be large. Especially in India, the largest democracy in the world (which also entails a large fraction of the population living below the poverty line), the State's decisions can leave many people struggling to survive.

Further, the assumption of a benevolent State too is exactly that, an assumption. The people in power want to remain in power. And sometimes they take shortcuts to do that. A popular way is to stifle dissent. It is wrong but is certainly effective. The State then introduces another variable which has to be factored in.

It is the trade-offs that States make which constantly form the subjects of many a debate. And it is here also, that the liberals become so important. Liberals take up the responsibility of being the nation's conscience. Of pointing out that the harm being done, even after being juxtaposed with the good being done, is not acceptable. The liberal points at the affected people and dredges out the uncomfortable truths that we would much rather ignore. The liberal fights, whines, snaps and ensures that the basic tenets of democracy do not just remain theories. For democracy means that we advance together as a people and the wants of the few do not outweigh the needs of the many.

The Apparent Conflict of Indian Liberalism

The last sentence regarding the needs and the wants is a fairly popular refrain from those of the communist persuasion. However, it would be a mistake to call the idea of liberalism a leftist one. Of course, some of the ideas and the inspirations are common to both ideologies. But that does not mean that one is the subset of the other. In fact, a simple and inherent differentiation between the communists and the liberals is that communists want the State to regulate things while liberals would ideally want the State to stay out of the individual's life.

This brings us to an apparent conflict of Indian liberalism. While Indian liberals will shout themselves hoarse about the right of an individual to do as they please, the very same liberals expect the State to actively support those in acute need. So, what is that they want? State or no State? Should the State interfere in the lives of the citizens or not?

The answer to these questions is the same as the one to life's other important questions. And that is, 'it depends'. There are simply too many variables involved to give a yes or no answer. The State has to step in for people in dire need. The poor require the State's support to cross the poverty line and to live a better life. The State must step in and fight epidemics. The State must take control of the public goods and ensure a fair distribution of them.

What is not required or wanted is the State stepping into the lives and trampling upon the freedom of the people who don't need it. And quite frankly, no one needs the State to trample on their rights.

A Simplified Position

The position of liberalism thus stands simplified. Liberals are not advocates of the anarchist theory which demands that there be no State. They recognise that an institution dedicated to the betterment of the people, which also has the power to fulfil its objectives, is extremely important and can be an instrument of tremendous good. The State has a crucial role in collectively developing the resources available to the nation and to ensure that those who have been born or fallen into poverty get the chance to rise.

What liberals are against is the interference with personal freedoms. And this is what really defines liberalism. The State cannot be allowed to make rules which infringe on these freedoms. In other words, while the State is certainly allowed and indeed required to affect the larger societal environment so as to ensure conditions conducive to the growth of its citizens, it cannot go into private lives and tell people what to do or what to think. It is from these canons or commandments that the liberal position on most issues can be derived.

One of the simplest examples for this is the right to privacy. It is a right heavily debated in the world as well as in India. The State has sought to enter into the lives of the citizens and to, for the lack of a better word, snoop on them. It has instituted the Aadhaar scheme which requires you to register with all your personal details. It is theoretically voluntary but as the State has instituted many schemes which need your Aadhaar card, it is now bordering on the compulsory. Liberals have risen against the scheme as it means that the State is privy to the citizens' private details which might not have been shared otherwise. It is making the citizen do something which they might not otherwise.

This could be another way to define liberalism. A liberal would be against the State making people do something they would not want to ordinarily. It is not a perfect definition as it would have to come with the necessary exceptions which would apply to criminals or people who do not care about the society as a whole. However, it does shed some light on the way a liberal thinks.

Another example is the right to free speech. There have been multiple occasions in history when a government which wants to stay in power has stifled all dissent. You cannot lose if you have no opponent. These governments have often faced their fiercest opponents in liberals. Liberals cannot bear the thought of dissent or indeed any speech being muzzled. This is why liberals protested loudly when books by Salman Rushdie, Taslima Nasreen and Wendy Doniger were banned.

Liberals have taken that famous Voltaire quote to heart: "They may not agree with what you say, but they will fight to death to defend your right to say it". Liberals are ready to defend their ideas and there are many who relish the challenge, the opportunity to test their beliefs against on the anvil of a well-reasoned debate. And debates can only take place in a society which permits free speech.

Liberals will always push for a society which allows citizens to speak their minds regardless of whether they agree with them.

The debate on pornography gives another example of liberal thinking. Regardless of whether a liberal watches pornography, they recognise the right of the people to do what they please in their own homes as long as it doesn't harm others. Thus, you will find numerous liberals fighting the State when it seeks to ban pornography. The core idea is to let people exercise their individual freedom to the fullest possible extent.

Even where liberals demand State intervention (say, while pushing for a dam which will provide electricity for a lot of people), they put in riders to ensure the welfare of those affected. So, in a rehabilitation debate for people affected by a development project, liberals would insist on involving those people in the discussions so that they can get what they want, instead of getting what the State thinks is best for them.

Who are the Liberals?

Till now the discussion has centred on what liberals do and how they think. It is also important to understand where they come from. Thus even though they come from all walks of life, some population groups are more represented than others.

One of the common characteristics shared by many Indian liberals is a college education, usually in the humanities. A majority of them are social workers, journalists, lawyers and teachers. They have had their ideas shaped by much discussion as their education is largely centred on conversations.

This is also the basis of the most common allegation levelled against the liberals. It is that of elitism. For it is true that, it is in the universities and the urban landscapes that liberals have flourished. In contrast, rarely have the rural areas, where poverty reigns supreme, thrown up the defenders of personal freedoms. This is because the priorities that govern these people are different. An upbringing in cities and a graduate degree will usually ensure that one never has to worry about the basic needs of life like food, electricity or even a toilet. The migrant farmer on the other hand has had to work day and night for all those things before even starting to contemplate what individual freedoms might entail.

As the wealthy have dominated the liberal ranks, it is but natural that it is their concerns which are foremost in the liberal agenda. Therefore, the ideas of free markets and private property, which would allow the wealthy to retain their riches, find much support in liberalism. What the poor man gets are a few lines in the Constitution, guaranteeing him equality and a right life. The liberals will push for equality but will balk at the idea of separate representation for what are in fact, a separate people. Absolute equality in the current conditions is strived for without regard to the unequal pasts we have seen.

Conclusion

The idea of liberalism is thus not a perfect one. Except there is no single idea of liberalism! And that is what makes it a good and workable philosophy. Its flexibility ensures that it can be moulded to suit different cultures and different nations unlike say, communism.

Perhaps a simple way to summarise the liberal position is "Live and Let Live". Or even "Live and Let Die" (keeping in mind the numerous liberals on the pro-euthanasia side). The idea of individual freedom is the very essence of the philosophy. Liberals believe that the individual is capable of doing great things. And sometimes not so great things, depending on what they feel like doing that day. Liberalism merely asks for the right for the individuals to do as they please. They want the State to live on, for it has many benefits. But it also wants the State to leave its citizens alone until absolutely necessary. Hence, their simple request to those worthy people who hold the power to influence what the State does is—live and let live.

15

VAGEESHA SUSHAN

Liberty *versus* Liberalism: Defending the Freedom of Expression

Liberal, a term that was attested to me for the first time in summer of 2009 when I was in class IX. I remember it had been a sunny day, the skies blue in their rapture, ignorant and uncaring of the heat that scorched us ninth graders. There in class where overworked fans had continued their motion, a very interested teacher had hurled questions after questions on me for the very fact that I refused to back down.

I had been defending the freedom of expression by stating that Salman Rushdie had every right to write *Satanic Verses* and Tasleema Nasreen's *Lajja* was an invigorating fictional account of what she deemed went on in Bangladeshi society.

If you are wondering I got scolded by the teacher then you are wrong. What happened was even bizarre and it itched itself in my brain with a tenacity of remaining there forever.

My friend stood up, a friend I had known from the tender age of 6 and she literally told me to shut up. She said, and I am quoting it verbatim, "Freedom of expression doesn't mean anyone can hurt my religious feelings. What those books are is a work of heresy and all they do is to blaspheme the very foundation of my society and religion".

Imagine my surprise and disappointment.

I wasn't very world wise or well read in matters of religion and politics, and I couldn't understand how the fictional Gibreel Farishta and Salauddin Chamcha could hurt my friend's religious sentiments.

You can envisage the fate of my friendship. The friend who once had been my secret keeper was suddenly a stranger.

So I came to know, courtesy of those days that being very liberal in your ideas and attitudes didn't win you any points or friends for that matter.

The idea of liberty is a very appealing one but being a liberal, now that is not everyone's cup of tea, in fact, people find the label quite unacceptable.

In a society riddled with age old ideas of what to do and what not to do, what is right and what is wrong; us liberals appear as anomalies. We don't preach something and follow something else; we don't have two faces on a matter and somewhere in there confounded hearts the majority members of this society want liberals dissected in laboratory to find the cause of such diverse thinking. The *Satanic Verses* affair taught me that a human can't tolerate anything that is different from the very idea he holds as truth.

He hates what he doesn't understand.

Being a liberal doesn't mean I support anarchy. I believe in liberty with reasonable restrictions. Restrictions that make sure that I don't violate someone else's liberty. If we want to determine what a liberal is in couple of words, I would say that a liberal is one who believes in greater freedom for individual men.

Being a liberal in India doesn't mean I am Maoist or Naxal. No, what I am is a citizen of this nation like any other who just is very vocal about the issues and what she believes in. I have found that religion, caste, language, creed—they are personal issues. They shouldn't be colour coated and presented to the masses as a collective idea.

Supporting freedom of expression by stating that Salman Rushdie didn't do any wrong by writing *Satanic Verses* doesn't make me anti-Islamic. Or liking Ravi Verma's paintings doesn't make me anti-Hindu. Reading *Da Vinci Code* and believing that Jesus was married doesn't negate his greatness.

Why do we try to impose our ideas, our beliefs on someone else by giving it a label of truth?

The LGBT issues that have detonated a series of serious debates over the rights of these communities aren't anti-society. Supporting the LGBT community or welcoming the U.S. Supreme Court's decision in Obergefell *vs.* Hodges on legalising same sex marriage or criticising the Indian apex court for criminalising homosexuality isn't insanity. As a liberal, I believe in the basic human dignity that every individual born on this earth is entitled to. I believe in equality.

It's very easy to sit in studios and debate whether the decision of the apex court was right or wrong in India but it is very hard to publicaly proclaim that you don't see any immorality in homosexual relationships.

We Indians are very proud of our culture, heritage, language and legacy but beneath that we fail to see the rot that some of us have cultivated. Does our culture guide us to hate all those who are different? Does it state that we have to make everyone follow what we believe in?

As an Indian liberal I don't think I am an elite but an endangered species, for everyone wants to bag my head for their metaphorical wall.

When I proclaim that girls in Haryana too have the right to choose their life partners, I open myself for numerous attacks by so called 'bahubaalis' on my 'Indianity' and my faith in my culture.

If Raja Ram Mohan Roy wouldn't have questioned the age old archaic barbarism like *sati* and hadn't dared to profess the need for educating women, I wouldn't have been writing this essay rather I would have been trying to feed my rug rats.

So liberals, my friends, they question the things. They don't accept something just because our forefathers deemed it to be true. They don't imitate an idea, just because it comes from the West, the hub of liberal thinking.

If that would have been so, our traditions would have died long ago, and we would have lost our identity in our race to be like everyone else.

Being a liberal in this country also guarantees that sometime or other you get pelted with stones, eggs, rotten tomatoes and some things I would rather not write about. If you are incredibly lucky, you might just escape with a very scathing criticism directed at you.

I don't write it for sake of writing. Just like people don't mispronounce my name for the fact that they read it wrong. They do so because they want a chance to know what my name means and why despite belonging to a particular religion, my name doesn't reflect it.

My name is not a traditional name, so people generally enquire after my religion and when they utter that question, I can see that calculation going on in their eyes, the subtle shift of a complex thought process where they debate the pros and cons of my being in their religion or in some other religion.

Just like when they watch me enter a church, all they ask me when I come out is why I worship god of some other religion.

Does it concern them?

No, but yet they make faces when I proclaim that I believe in god but not religion.

Liberty looks quite fascinating in the Constitution, like a girl next door, whose face resonates in your mind and you don't care for the fact that you don't know what the girl is like.

I wonder what our Constitution makers had thought when they had included liberty in our Constitution. Had they envisioned how one day the lady liberty would be raped by the very heinous 'emergency' or how her children would be hunted like pair of elks.

India, the largest democracy we boast and yet have we ever wondered what kind of leaders we choose? We give them sweeping majorities but do we ever care for a faint liberal voice that gets trampled under the very eager feet of masses going to vote.

Indians have a very bad habit of condemning liberalism.

They forget that if liberalism is a panorama of freedom of self then once it also was the baton of rebellion. The same people who don't associate with different thinking approach praise the liberalisation of our markets that enriches and deepens their pockets.

Aren't they the 'hypocrites' and us 'fools'?

As a liberal, I vehemently support the fact that every human has freedom to state what he wants to and do what he desires to within the ambient parameters of our esteemed Constitution. By supporting liberty, I don't support the deaths of thousand innocents who die in some mad man's idiotic quest of finding his own identity or some extremist's perverse pleasure of believing in his cause.

Being a liberal is an art in moderation in this country. You have to state your points but you also have to take care that you are not stepping on toes of so called conservatives who prefer to breathe in the age old dust of their decomposed thoughts.

I was watching *Satyamev Jayate* one day and in that they showed a clip wherein a renowned priest of Benaras quite proudly stated that he still believes in untouchability and he is quite adamant in those beliefs. He further went on to say that for him the Constitution is nothing but a pile of pages stating bullshit as the Constitution hasn't been written according to the specifications of his holy scripture.

What would our Constitution makers say if their poor souls heard this even by mistake? Had they ever thought when they were writing Article 21 that liberty could be insulted like this?

Conservatives blame liberals and yet every time they open their mouths to spew any such nonsense, they are using their personal liberty. In India they can get away with anything and yet liberals are the ones at fault for stating something rational different than conservative rationality.

Had Raja Ram Mohan Roy faced such tribulations? Had Mahadev Govind Ranade?

Being liberal is barely tolerated in this country but I am not ashamed to be one.

I envision a society where liberty births intelligence and intellect. I wish for a society where a liberal is heard and not ignored; a society that celebrates the passion of someone like M.F. Husain, literary genius of Rushdie, and words of Nasreen that beg to be understood.

Liberalism is not a disease, nor is it contagious.

It's just a state of being who you are and what you believe in. I wish one day if a student stands to defend Rushdie, Nasreen or Ravi Verma, no one interrupts her to say that liberty is nothing but a woman in chains begging to be freed.

16

VAISHNAVI RAY

A Letter to 'I'

Dear 'I' who's being told,

I was sitting by my window last night and blogging about the pros and cons of legalising prostitution, when my phone showed a pop up 'Quote of the Day'. Somehow, what flashed on the screen seemed to strike a chord.

> When the people fear the government, there is tyranny.
> When the government fears the people, there is liberty.
>
> —Thomas Jefferson

So much for voicing basic freedom, I contemplated. I was a mixed bag of feelings. A string of fleeting thoughts started to run through my mind, like those whistle-stop jet trains.

If he is doing it, why not me? Should I do it? Am I doing it? IT? What is 'it'? And amidst this deluge of dubiety, the 'I' came into picture. Let me tell you that the 'I' you're imagining this minute isn't the 'I' who's writing this, but the 'I' who's being told.

As a kid, I always got dropped to school by daddy. And before entering the school gate came a time when all parents bid farewell to their kids. Some would hug their child, some would reprimand, some others would advise them not to cry, while my dad always had one thing to say, "Have fun, kiddo! And remember, no fighting; you say or do something because you believe you are right, but same with others. So, respect everyone's opinions and be a good girl. And you know who to talk to if there is a problem, don't you?"

I am 19 today, and I can vouch for the fact that this is undoubtedly the coolest advice someone has ever given me. My parents are avid readers, and thus haven't left a stone unturned to make me as wise as they could. The reason I like quoting a lot of people is because my dad always did.

As he read the newspaper each morning, he would make me sit on his lap and give me insights into what was happening world over. Then, he would ask me to sift right from wrong, educate me about my rights, tell me if what I was thinking was appropriate for the larger benefit of mankind, teach me that it was okay to have my opinion, but never disrespect another's and harm his/her sentiments. He would say, "It is not the power of doing what we like that is liberating, rather what we ought to." That, for me, is liberty. It feels good to know that my dad has always been a liberal, but never knew it.

As I grew older, dad asked me to take to reading and public speaking. Thus, I signed up for the public speaking class in my neighbourhood and took to believing that reading sets a person free. However, I remember the first time I saw a really huge book was when my mom was reading *Fountainhead*. She really liked Ayn Rand and always told me that Ayn Rand knows that a real revolution starts in men's minds and not on the streets. Today, I realise that Ayn Rand and many other esteemed writers like her preached libertarianism with every fibre of their being.

So, what for me, is liberty? Private property? Cooperative ownership? Limited government? Women's rights? Yes, it is all of this and beyond. Most importantly, liberty is 'freedom'. What then is freedom? The power to live as one wishes, a mere culmination of basic human rights. Let us not forget that among those rights, are the right to speak freely and the right to be heard, the right to emphasise political freedom and maximise autonomy, the right to indulge in voluntary association and primacy of individual judgement.

This philosophical belief in freedom also involves transcending the several boundaries that tend to unknowingly grip you and make you inattentive to the infected social atmosphere you continually inhale. Boundaries like expressing sexual freedom which is a direct expression of individual sovereignty and free love but sadly does not hold prevalence in most countries, and others like the revolting disparity between rich and poor, great and small, healthy and diseased. John Lennon said, "It doesn't matter how long my hair is or what colour my skin is or whether I am a woman or a man." I cannot disagree.

This one day, I saw the maid next door being tortured by her owner. She was 15 years old. I wondered what circumstances led her to this plight. I wished to do something about it. I told my mom I did not like what I saw. That minute, my mom realised that it was time to act. She realised that if I, a 17 year old, did not appreciate it; it is time for her, a 54 year old to introspect. The next thing I knew, she made some quick calls, and the police arrested my neighbours. Whoever said, "You can't marginalise more than half of the world's population and expect to see any meaningful solutions to the problems that aid the world".

It was then that I realised that sometimes, what you're most afraid of doing is the very thing that will set you free. I never looked back ever since. I have always stood up for what I believe, as long as it didn't hurt someone's sentiments.

I stood up against slavery when I liberated that 15 year old maid.

I stood up against corruption when I refused to bribe the local officer for my license.

I stood up against illiteracy when I urged my mom to educate my watchman's daughter.

I stood up against gender policing when I enlightened my uncle about why he shouldn't save up for the dowry of his daughter's marriage.

I stood up for my right to speech when I started the Public Speaking society of my university.

I stood up for liberty when I realised that there is a reason we are all different.

Like Ronald Reagan said, "Freedom is the right to question and change the established way of doing things." And that is what I've grown up to believe.

For in the end, liberty is a personal and lonely battle that only the brave and the mighty fight.

Love,

I, the advocate of liberty.

17

VANI MANCHANDA

Overcoming Disparity: Liberty for All

> I would say that, as long-term institutions, I am totally against dictatorships. But a dictatorship may be a necessary system for a transitional period. At times it is necessary for a country to have, for a time, some form or other of dictatorial power. As you will understand, it is possible for a dictator to govern in a liberal way. And it is also possible for a democracy to govern with a total lack of liberalism. Personally I prefer a liberal dictator to a democratic government lacking liberalism.
>
> —Friedrich August von Hayek

In the late 18th century, the famous American and French Revolutions sought the same primary goal—'liberty'. Those who fought in these two different rebellions were contesting the same kind of repressive rule as well—'Authoritarian', albeit in slightly different forms. The denotation of 'liberalism' that followed in the 19th and 20th centuries directly originated from these upheavals as well as from the Age of Enlightenment, which propagated reason and individual rights, instead of traditional sovereignty.

But what distinguished liberals from the revolutionaries and the philosophers was the emphasis on individuality instead of equality, and on personal freedom of action and thought instead of that of the masses. This was the articulation of liberalism in its most bona fide form, as worded by the English philosopher, John Stuart Mill. From the phenomenon of the Industrial Revolution and the experience of the illustrious middle-class that was a part of it—individual freedom to pursue private interests was perceived beneficial not just to the advancement of business and civilisation, but also for good governance, and eventually, human happiness. Liberalism, essentially, placed such personal freedom above unity of community, and even the nation.

Theoretically, this concept may seem appealing to some as the ideal state of affairs. But realistically, it is not viable since human beings do not actually possess the high degree of inherent rationality and goodness that pure liberalists boast them to. Simply put, if everyone has the unrestricted right to do whatever he or she wants to, there will be utter chaos and lawlessness. Thankfully, this realisation was followed by the birth of Classical Liberalism in the 19th century, which is the understanding that most people draw from the term liberalism today. It advocated a particular type of society with specific civil liberties such as the right to property; economic freedom; a certain degree of equality and freedom of press; and political independence through an elected, representative form of government, aka democracy and suffrage. Post then, dozens of countries have revolted to become free of repressive authoritarian control, and liberate their people to become democracies, of which India was one. But despite being a sovereign, socialist, secular, democratic republic since 65 years, are India's people truly liberal? If no, why, and if yes, to what degree and in what sense?

Liberalism, in its entirety, has become a very broad concept with extensions and branches in numerous schools of politics, society, economics, religion, culture, and of course, philosophy. But Indian liberalism, in my opinion, can be very succinctly characterised by just three words—pseudo, exclusive, and misinterpreted.

India has come a long way since independence, and has opened up quite a bit in all the progressive disciplines stated earlier. But rapid population growth since then, totalling 1.25 billion today with close to 70 per cent of that still concentrated in rural or underdeveloped areas, has allowed change to take effect slowly—rather, very slowly. The land of villages is also a land of reverent religions and countless long-standing traditions and customs. The British rule and increasingly unfurling education has diminished many of the most dreadful cultural practices, but unfortunately, a lot of them still remain in either their totality or in different forms. The intention of the Constitution makers to be politically correct and just, without accounting for the extent of prevailing backwardness, led to the unabridged and rampant liberty of religion and cultural conventions, in turn making India less liberal at the core.

Now, you may argue that liberalisation of religion is actually an integral part of civil freedom as a whole, and in saying that you would be absolutely correct. The freedom to follow any desired religion is indeed a part of liberalism. But with such predominance of regressive religion and ethnic practices, authentic liberalism can never flourish. There is no real freedom of thought and action when most Indians are so highly influenced by, the more often than not, ridiculous words and teachings of spiritual leaders that they fail to think rationally for themselves. There is no equality in religion and culture when there is still widespread female infanticide, discrimination against women, and the castes. And there is no economic freedom as well in religion when it is tied to issues like birth control.

To make matters more convoluted, religion has been liberally conjoined with political and business agendas to deceive and divide the Indian society with the intention of earning votes and profits. Even the right to democratically elected representation seems severely tainted and pre-selected when you contemplate the extent of family ties in politics, prevalent in nearly every national government. These outlooks seem to endow an extremely pseudo facet to two of the most important liberties that our predecessors struggled for and that we 'supposedly' enjoy today.

No one can repudiate the elite hallmark of Indian liberalism, marked thoroughly by all possible forms of privilege—cast, class, geography, education, even the colour of skin, and so on. This grants the liberals in India a seat on top of the broad pyramid of exclusion that is guaranteed to create bitterness in those who do not share the benefits that the liberals so easily take for granted. This discontentment and crossness of being ostracised from such exclusivities doesn't take long to turn into deprivation the farther one moves from the metropolises, where rabble-rousers lie in ready wait to burgeon the seeds of disfavour among the unprivileged and secure their vote banks for anything but a liberal regime.

Being a liberal in India, thus, has a different connotation attached to it based on how entitled one is. If you ask someone who is part of the crest and upper-middle part of societal hierarchy, they'll most likely explain liberalism in its most naked sense—openness and the personal freedom of expression and action. They may also add to that in such that the most liberal countries harbour the most satisfied citizens. Move to or below the middle of this hierarchy and the ideology takes on different meanings and additions—the right to egalitarianism, fairness, and justice in all spheres of life.

This disparity comes as no surprise considering that the elitism of liberals is supplemented by their indifference to economic equality as a principle due to liberalism's innate connection with laissez-faire capitalism. Unable to even engage in any sort of consequential chit-chat dealing with such social inequality and exploitation, Indian liberalism would rather safeguard its inherited advantages than to cease deploring and accept responsibility for the communalist and fascist vermin that it itself has brought about. In other words, the true aim of the highly exclusive liberalism in India seems to be the foreclosure of any hope of social transformation that would enable access to liberty for all.

The plenitude of Indians will agree with the reality that their fates are more or less sealed the day they are born into Indian society. What they will eat, wear, think, and study; to whom they will pray and get married; who they have to be better than, as well as where they should study and work; almost everything in their upcoming lives is laid out like a meticulous business plan before they even have the capacity to understand what the word choice is. And things could be even worse if the child happens to be born a female regardless of the parents' position in the hierarchy of society. Hence, most new *Bharatvasis* are seemingly inducted into tradition and conservatism right at the onset, which causes them to misunderstand the term liberal through their developing and learning years.

You may inculpate it as a shortcoming of the education system or of a restrictively orthodox culture, but nonetheless, the ambitious Indian youth comprehends liberalism with the same blemished lens, as once did the middle-class of the Industrial Revolution, and now does the select class of Indian liberals—the freedom to do and say whatever they want. Some would advocate this interpretation to an expression of individuality and freedom of choices. However, such is not the individuality that was stood up for during the times of enlightenment and revolution, which held some regard for how it could affect the lives of those around them. Today's misinterpretation of this personal expression shows no such regard, wherein violence, DUIs, rape, and bigotry have become commonplace among even teenagers, who also exhibit exemplary confidence of ultimately being absolved of any responsibility for related incidents. Being liberal is, unfortunately, confused with being unnecessarily rebellious, and heeding no words or logic other than one's own.

A hoary old question has been that after so many years of being a liberal democracy, is a richer, more capitalist economy bound to emerge in India? Possibly, yes. But only if India and its people can truly be designated the title of liberal, and that too in all the correct senses. Even though liberalist ideas can provide some of the most lucid answers to many of India's tribulations, the previously presented arguments opine that the country still has ways to go from actually being liberal. Even in the economic arena, discretionary powers need to be plucked from substandard bureaucrats and politicians; the state made smaller; and the markets allowed greater freedom and openness in allocating resources. Indian media also calls for a greater degree of freedom from political and business propaganda, but at the same time needs to be more socially responsible as well as a little intelligent about what content it chooses to inform and mislead people with.

Just like too much or too little salt in food can make it inedible, a disproportionate excess or sparseness of any ideology can lead to chronic disorderliness. Rather, a certain balance between the various elements of liberty and long-standing opposing culture is necessary to tone down the overly restrictive nature of society, in order to encourage open-mindedness and free thought, rather than the misinterpretation of civil and personal freedom.

The threats to individual freedom are ever present making it necessary for freedom loving individuals to organise for civil liberties and constantly explore new channels for the expression of critical thought. In the long perspective of Indian history and tradition concern for the individual and his rights has been conspicuous by its absence. India can progress on the lines indicated in the Constitution only through a break with the dead past.

Though, the exact recipe for that equilibrium is not an established formula and needs to be experimented with. A more liberal and open India may indeed develop one day, but not before a light is shone into the dreary corners that currently make it artificial, private, and misconstrued.

18

PRAKHAR MISRA

Liberalism in India: The Lucifer Effect

India is like islands of New York in a sea of Sub-Saharan Africa.

—Amartya Sen

The Lucifer Effect

To analyse any fundamental theoretical argument, one needs to explain the context in which the theory is being looked at. Given that we're talking about India, it only makes sense to bring in ideas that can better explain the current scenario adequately so that we can absorb the ongoing events in a disciplined manner. It is interesting that I start my explanation about India by mentioning something that happened 7 seas away—in the USA.

In 1971, a psychologist at Stanford University by the name of Philip Zimbardo modulated an experiment to understand and learn the effects of prisons on prisoners. This, rather infamous experiment was the Stanford Prison Experiment[1] where randomly chosen graduate-students studying at Stanford University were selected and bundled into 2 groups—one of the jailers/prison—guards and the other of the prisoners. The experiment was designed for 2 weeks time, but it had to be shut down within a week primarily because the roles of the guards and prisoners had been taken too seriously. During the experiment, the guards tortured prisoners mindlessly to the extent that some of them quit the experiment within a day or 2. Some prisoners gave a hard time to the other prisoners at the insistence of the guards, exactly like it happens in real prison cells. Psychological torture, authoritarian rule, rampant abuse and beyond

1. Zimbardo, P., C. Hanning, W. Curtis Banks, D. Jaffe (1971). *Stanford Prison Experiment: A Simulation Study of the Psychology of Imprisonment.* Conducted at Stanford University. August.

the line harassment are some of the terms used to describe the effects of the experiment. This was within 6 days of assuming the roles of the prisoners/guards by very normal, everyday-going Stanford students.

In his book *The Lucifer Effect*, Zimbardo talks about this experiment as the effect that created Satan out of God's beloved angel Lucifer when Gabriel, the arch-angel expelled Lucifer from Heaven. It was Lucifer indeed who transformed into Satan and created Hell after the expulsion. The experiment tells us that people are not evil intrinsically or culturally. Their reactions very largely depend on the environment they are exposed to. Moreover, the experiment confirms that the reaction of people can be completely opposite to what it is expected to be given a shift in the environment by the same degree. People are so heavily under the influence of their environment that they forget who they really are and what they themselves believe in. And that is the tyranny of the human mind across all races, religions and countries too—India included.

To my mind—this is exactly what explains the 'Modi Wave' that took the country away and which has since then influenced umpteen number of people into an ideology of 'Hindutva', it itself endorses. This has, as a consequence of the recent change in ideological beliefs, led to a decline in liberal thought. In very common parlance—if everyone around me believes in extremities, I might as well do so too.

Narendra Modi's speeches while standing up for elections and creating the Modi wave reflected a lot of extremism in them. 'Bomb Pakistan', 'Jail corrupt politicians', 'Bring back black money' were all ways to mould a dialogue with the public telling them that the tolerance levels have crossed the bar and thus strong actions need to be taken to bring things under control.

Liberal thought was missing from his speeches, and therefore from the minds of the voters. The problem is that even the opposition missed out on the middle-ground of being liberal and set itself on the other side of the spectrum. The Lucifer effect set in and people went with the flow of thought denying the right of any other approach to even exist. The 'what-is-everybody-doing-I-should-do-too' syndrome caught on very easily and was further reflected in Arvind Kejriwal's speeches while running for the post of the Delhi Chief Minister.

In India, liberal thought never really seeped through to the masses—it was always looked upon as an elitist idea. This coupled with the Lucifer effect has led to a decline of such discourse, limited only to platforms like Facebook and Twitter, acutely non-representative of the level at which such discourses should be engaged in.

Answering Impatience with Economics and Religion

The common masses sense frustrations across the spectrum in their daily lives. They, therefore, look forward to a certain 'godly' figure to give them the answers. The constant need for this one answer is restored by the agony caused by frustrations of each day—multiplying the need and decreasing patience levels. Therefore, the solution to this problem is taken up in patronising an answer in the name of god. Hinduism, more than any other religion sees this in the light of current events, for there is not one god but many—each to satisfy a different curiosity.

It was pen-down that God made Eve by breaking Adam's rib. This, very subtle 'difference' in the two genders was given a hierarchical dimension, thus giving rise to patriarchy for it was interpreted as because of Adam—Eve was made—therefore Adam is the leader and Eve the follower. Today's India also sees something similar happening. Differences in the society are re-interpreted as hierarchical differences and thus begin the saga of who is above whom—in effect answering the question of who really has all the answers—the 'godly' figure that we're looking for.

Since market capitalism has taken over, ideas of compensating for oppressed behaviour, redistribution etc., are fading away in India. The prominent agenda seems to be that of 'development'. We see people day in and day out talking about this—in political parties, coffee-table conversations and even in the media. What we don't see is the subtle link between the economic idea of capitalism, which as believed will create jobs and lead to development; and the religious ideology of 'Hindutva' which tries to create a separate identity sounding progressive with its linkage to economic capitalism but otherwise embedded with the notion of creating a hierarchical system.[2]

The liberal thought is more of a 'think-and-see-for-yourself' idea, something that doesn't quite fly with the impatient masses that are trying to look for hope of a better future in every nook and corner. In today's dynamic world, nobody quite has the time to discuss and deliberate these issues. They instead are looking for an all-answering supra individual to satisfy their thirst. In such an environment, liberal thought often gets lost and crowded out by market forces and religious intellectuals.

Thus, we see the rise of a new faith in yet another individual to take us all to the 'promised land'. This faith further prevents the liberal thought to make its point to the masses.

Historical Perspectives

The position of liberalism today in India, and therefore that of a liberal, has a lot to do with its past proponents and sustenance of the philosophy of liberalism.

Raja Ram Mohan Roy was described as "the bridge over which India passed from her unmeasured past into her incalculable future."[3] As his successors took the baton forward, they seemed only to have moved into a silo, being distant form the Indian masses. Dadabhai Naoroji, Mahadeo Govind Ranade, Gopal Krishna Gokhale weren't peoples' men. All of them had sought to reason out the happenings and events during their times and then do what is right, but they couldn't percolate the same approach of thinking to the people. They were, thence, regarded as elitist and were looked up to; but in no way would common middle class people fill in their footsteps voluntarily.

Liberalism as a philosophy grew during the 'Reformation' in Europe, primarily as a positive revolution against the 2 oppressors—the state and the church. While John Locke was the 'prophet of Liberalism', in effect it was "a by-product of the effort of the middle

2. This idea stemmed from a conversation with my Economics professor, Indradeep Ghosh and therefore the credit goes to him to have seen this argument through to the very end, so as to allow me to understand it and then use it for this essay.

3. Collet, S. (1914). *The Life and Letters of Raja Rammohun Roy*. Calcutta.

class to win its place in the sun."[4] The Indian interpretation was, however, not fighting against the Church or the State, but against superstitions and dogmas that existed within the Indian society and continue to exist in the present times.

At the end of his speech on the Elementary Education Bill in 1912, Gopal Krishna Gokhale, a leading intellectual of liberal thought said:

> Moreover, I have always felt and have often said that we, of the present generation in India, can only hope to serve our country by our failures. The men and women who will be privileged to serve her by their successes will come later. We must be content to accept cheerfully the place that has been allotted to us in our onward march. This Bill, thrown out today, will come back again and again, till on the stepping-stones of its dead selves, a measure ultimately rises which will spread the light of knowledge throughout the land.[5]

The Right to Education Act was passed in 2009 to be inacted in 2010, something that Gokhale had proposed a century ago. He was also right in maintaining that the bill will come back again and again until it is passed. This is the legacy of liberal thought that needs to be venerated in present times.

In the same speech Gokhale also mentions, "We shall be entitled to feel that we have done our duty, and where the call of duty is clear, it is better even to labour and fail than not to labour at all." This is exactly what the Indian liberals feel even today. More than a century has gone past us and still liberal thought has progressed to little avail in this country. But, like Gokhale mentions—liberals can only hope to serve the country by their failures, a thought that has taken a shape so dangerous that it requires one to sacrifice their life and fail, in order to be successful.

---

4. Yack, B. (1996). *Liberalism Without Illusions: Essays on Liberal Theory and the Political Vision of Judith N. Shklar.* University of Chicago Press.
5. Gopal Krishna Gokhale's Speech on the Elementary Education Bill at the Imperial Legislative Council on 18 March 1912.

In the Light of the day

In times as recent as the past month, the Government of India under the leadership of the omnipotent figure of Narendra Modi has become paternalistic in its approach. From food habits to voicing opinions against individuals—the government has tried to curb the advent of thought, which leads to healthy discourse. It has rather given a unilateral dimension to any issue arising within the public by justifying its worth as the protector of the Indian culture. It has projected an image that only those subscribing to the ideology of what it wants to propagate are nationalistic and patriotic. Everyone else is then labelled as an anti-Indian and therefore their thoughts are subdued before even being vented out in domains of consequence.

A Liberal therefore faces the question, 'who will regulate the regulator?'. We see this question validating itself in Maharashtra (having the same ruling party as that at the Union) when it recently came out with a circular, which allows the police to arrest people on sedition charges under Section 124A of the IPC. For section 124A to be invoked, the circular states, "words, signs or representations must bring the government into hatred or contempt must cause or attempt to cause dissatisfaction, enmity and disloyalty to the government." Today's state governments are not open to varying viewpoints but instead have a prepared agenda by which they vow to not deviate.

The pushing of the one-point agenda of 'Hindutva' is also clear in the appointment of the ministers. All cabinet ministers and the prime minister have been a part of the Rashtriya Swayamsevak Sangh (RSS) either as a 'Swayamsevak' or as a 'Pracharak'. Moreso, the boundaries are crossed when the devotion to the common ideology becomes a metric to select a person for a certain post rather than his/her capabilities to do justice to the seat being awarded. This was seen when Gajendra Chauhan, a below-par actor, was selected as the director of the country's premier Film Institute. With him, a couple other RSS followers were named as a part of the board of the institute. While, instead of them—more credible replacements could be made—the state made no attempt to change its thinking on this, even after umpteen protests by students and faculty alike.

The primacy for the individual in all walks of life is what a liberal would argue for. It seems downright bad for the country if merit is being discounted and replaced by one's faiths and beliefs. The liberal thought would never argue for the favour of such an action and the fact that liberals themselves are being ridiculed is enough to create an environment where this is slowly washed away.

A ban on watching porn and a ban on eating beef and a ban on comedy shows etc., is nowhere close to the idea of a 'limited government'. Such paternalistic behaviour is what further subsides liberal thought. There is no sprouting of ideas that can challenge the government for its own good. It seems the state knows it all and knows it well.

But, the problem with this attitude becomes intolerable when people are murdered for having raised their voices against the government. The murder of M.M. Kalburgi, a rationalist and a liberal, by a Bajrang Dal (offshoot of the RSS) leader raises a question mark on the intentions of the government. The culprits haven't even been arrested[6] yet, leave alone being tried for their crimes. In fact, the Bajrang Dal leader tweeted saying his next target would be another liberal by the name of K.S. Bhagwan.[7] Very recently, a 75-year old Muslim scholar and literary critic, M.M. Basheer was given a death threat[8] to stop writing a column on *Ramayana* in a vernacular news daily.

Words fail to describe the anguish of a liberal in today's times in India. Being a liberal, it is but natural to allow individuals to indulge in the actions they intend for themselves but if that is exactly what is killing liberal thought then a contradiction arises.

Liberalism today is no different than as it was in the 17th and the 18th century. As Parth J. Shah describes in his essay[9] the times of Raja

---

6. *http://www.thehindu.com/news/national/karnataka/kalburgis-murder-arrest-the-culprits/article762 7479.ece.*
7. *http://www.ndtv.com/india-news/striking-similarity-in-murders-of-dabholkar-pansare- kalburgi-congress-1213655.*
8. *http://www.huffingtonpost.in/2015/09/04/mm-basheer-ramayana_n_8086598.html.*
9. *http://ccs.in/evolution-liberalism-india.*

Ram Mohan Roy, Gopal Krishna Gokhale etc. saw liberalism as an attack on anti-life social practices like *sati* and remarriage.

Today's liberal is fighting the battle against the same evils in different forms, against the government, the society and mostly—against himself—questioning his own intentions and being aware to not let Lucifer step into his thought.

19

ROHIT BALAGOPAL

The Indian Liberal: Golden Age or Gilded Cage?

The curious lexicon of Internet slang today would have made George Orwell proud; from doublespeak to LOL, the unique contractions of the English language that feature heavily in his *1984* seem to have percolated through the vast nexus of the Interweb into reality.

However, the one word that truly remains a valuable addition to the English language floating in the sea of abbreviations, alliterations and emoticons that characterise modern web-speak is "facepalm". Essentially, a facepalm is the physical act of hitting ones forehead in sheer frustration at a display of idiocy that merits no other reaction.

Regrettably, a liberal Indian today is all too familiar with the urge to facepalm. Putting aside, the general jingoism that invariably surrounds India's much touted claim to being the world's largest democracy, the average liberal finds India a fickle blend of conservative roots masked by nearly pseudo libertarian sensibilities.

A melting pot of diverse cultures that possess a striking contrast in every aspect of social life cannot be held to the same yardstick,and to even apply the general idea (read Western idea) of libertarianism would be fallacious in every sense of the word. Providing a descriptive analyses here would serve no purpose than to bore the trousers off even a patient reader.

So, perhaps a story of modern libertarianism instead, might be more appropriate. Let us consider the history of India. After numerous invasions (the most recent being the British who colonised India and incredibly managed to keep a population of over a billion souls subjugated for over two centuries with a handful of white men and field artillery), India has always strived to adapt to the customs and ideals of her invaders. Unfortunately, while India's tacit compliance was able to allow the British to help introduce India to the wonder of 20th century industrial improvement; the bankers, merchants and later administrators of the East India Company also brought with them an exceedingly repressive Victorian morality that soon permeated every aspect of the Indian ethos.

Eventually, through a long awaited turn of events, Indians galvanised into action by years of racially-charged economic exploitation, decided to give Her Majesty's subjects their version of the bum's rush. Unfortunately, much like Icarus, hubris was their downfall and the liberals who had fought alongside them waited for the "stroke of the midnight hour" to turn India into a liberal state, soon had their hopes and dreams brutally crushed when they realised that they had basically traded British conservatism for Indian conservatism.

For over four decades after independence, India severed ties economically and closed itself off to the rest of the world, and while Britain soon traded Victorian morality for the liberalism of the sixties; India though free in the legal sense remained enmeshed in traditions that no longer could be said to exist with their erstwhile oppressors.

Any student of law in modern India is often baffled by the lack of recognition of issues such as marital rape or homosexuality in modern criminal jurisprudence (with the former being ignored and latter criminalised). Projects are written, essays are composed and eventually the poor law student still sees no change in the same. Little does our hapless bar aspirant know that for over four decades, such matters were never amended or even given due consideration. Law Commissions and reports soon fell prey to vote- bank politics and the laws remained the same. Issues such as this were merely swept under the rug as though they never existed in the first place. The much criticised US army policy of "Don't ask, don't tell" is remarkably effective when practiced by the second largest population on Earth.

Fear not, for this story does have a happy ending. It was the policy of liberalisation in the nineties following near economic collapse that saved our ideals. Our economy was in near shambles and the disaffected youth, fed up to the teeth with conservatism in every aspect of his life—from the "License Raj" of the State to the India-centric education of his school to the increasing social interference in his private life—took to the liberal ideals of Western thought and lifestyle like a certain aquatic avian to good old water.

Filled with an Indian education, they soon extrapolated the conveniently simple paradigms of the West to apply to many questions about their own lifestyle that had plagued them for decades. Like Gandhi, a liberal in his own right they too, refused to be blown off their feet by any (culture).

The modern Indian liberal is no longer tied to the shackles of a history with conservatism. Born after liberalisation, he has never known red-tapism, nepotism or conservatism as previous generations. The modern liberal enjoys access to the liberal ideas that flood the Internet as he is exposed to more cultures and paradigms than he could have ever conceived. That isn't to say that being a liberal is easy. His demons are tougher to destroy than his predecessor who fought a repressive State. His demons are the values of his family that he has been trained never to question, the views of his elders that he has been taught are absolute truths and finally, the sheer stupidity of those whose views are repressive in the extreme, but who enjoy the same right to speech as he does. Little wonder that, the true liberal is rare to find as to even qualify as a liberal, he must deconstruct everything he knows to explore which he perceives to be a truth and yet be willing to allow others to hold differing views. In a country with one of the largest youth populations, the liberal is everywhere, but the true liberal is a rare sight distinguished only by inquisitiveness and a scientific temperament to all aspects of life.

Coming back to the original question, who is a liberal in modern day India?

The religious boy, disregarding his instincts to conform and laughing over an illegally downloaded copy of the recently banned AIB Roast video is a liberal as much the Hindu who dissented with his family's belief to marry his Muslim sweetheart, as are the thousands of students who risked police brutality last year to protest against the draconian imposition of 66 A of the Information and Technology Act to enable censorship of free opinion on the Internet

Ultimately, the liberal is not a rebel for the sheer thrill of rebellion—his hallmark is tolerance and exploration, after all. But, the sign of an "Indian liberal" is to put aside one's religious beliefs for a minute to marvel at the stupidity of religious leaders who claim that using mobile phones causes an increase in rape.

Facepalm indeed.